First World War

and Army of Occupation

War Diary

France, Belgium and Germany

16 DIVISION
49 Infantry Brigade
Gloucestershire Regiment
18th (Service) Battalion
1 August 1918 - 31 May 1919

WO95/1977/1

The Naval & Military Press Ltd
www.nmarchive.com
Published in association with The National Archives

Published by

The Naval & Military Press Ltd

Unit 10 Ridgewood Industrial Park,

Uckfield, East Sussex,

TN22 5QE England

Tel: +44 (0) 1825 749494

www.naval-military-press.com

www.nmarchive.com

This diary has been reprinted in facsimile from the original. Any imperfections are inevitably reproduced and the quality may fall short of modern type and cartographic standards.

Contents

Document type	Place/Title	Date From	Date To
Heading	1977/1 18 Battalion Gloucestershire Regiment Aug 1918-May 1919		
Heading	16th Division 49th Infy Bde 18th Bn Gloucester Regt Aug 1918-May 1919 From UK		
War Diary		01/08/1918	30/09/1918
Operation(al) Order(s)	18th. Bn. The Gloucestershire Regiment Operation Order No. 13	10/09/1918	10/09/1918
War Diary		01/10/1918	31/10/1918
War Diary	In The Field	01/11/1918	31/12/1918
Miscellaneous	49th Inf. Bde. H.Q	04/02/1919	04/02/1919
War Diary		01/01/1919	31/01/1919
Heading	18 Gloucester Vol 7		
War Diary		01/02/1919	28/02/1919
War Diary	Mons-en-Pevele	01/03/1919	26/03/1919
War Diary	Bersee	27/03/1919	31/05/1919

1977/1

18 Battalion Gloucestershire Regiment

Aug 1918 – May 1919

16TH DIVISION
49TH INFY BDE

18TH BN GLOUCESTER REGT

AUG 1918-MAY 1919

From U K

48th Divn

Aug '18
May '19

Instructions regarding War Diaries and Intelligence Summaries are contained in F. S. Regs., Part II. and the Staff Manual respectively. Title pages will be prepared in manuscript.

18th Bn. Gloucester Regt

WAR DIARY
or
INTELLIGENCE SUMMARY.

(Erase heading not required.)

H9/16

Army Form C. 2118.

Vol 1

Place	Date	Hour	Summary of Events and Information	Remarks and references to Appendices
	1-8-18		The Battalion, less Transport, lands at Boulogne about 11.0am after a quiet and uneventful crossing. The Transport crossed over to LE HAVRE on July 30th. All arrangements were excellently made for the journey both in England and in France; the weather is perfect and all went delightfully smoothly. The total strength of the Battalion is 41 Officers, of whom one is left in charge of Details and will rejoin later, and 770 other ranks. A nominal roll of all the Officers who crossed over with the Battalion is attached. On arrival at Boulogne the Battalion is marched up to Ostrohove Rest Camp marching from the Quay at 11.30am. 25 men fell out. – and soon settles in comfortably enough. About 11.0pm a few enemy bombing machines appear and a few bombs are dropped, none within half a mile of our camp; some damage is done in the town.	
	2-8-18		The Battalion, less Transport, moves by rail to the Divisional Concentration Area in the neighbourhood of SAMER. The first half battalion entrains at 9.16am at the Central Station, the second following 3 hours later. After about an hour's journey we detrain at SAMER in pouring rain, most of the Transport is waiting at the station to take our baggage & packs, and we are soon on the march to our final destination HARINGHEN, about 5 miles away. On arrival we learn from the billeting party that there is not room in that village for the whole Battalion, and 'D' Company is therefore detached to the next village, HAUT PICHOT, about a mile away. Brigade Headquarters are at FRENCQ, some 4 miles distant, and the other Battalions of the Brigade are all in the neighbourhood. Lieut. H.N. PARKER is attached to the Brigade Staff as Assistant Staff Captain, from today.	
	3-8-18		The day is spent in settling in. The billets are indifferent and the great lack of water is a serious difficulty; this however is overcome with the help of a motor lorry which comes to us twice a day. A marquee is obtained for use as an Officers' Mess & we are just able to get everybody in it. Football and Boxing competitions are organised & general preparations made for the commencement of a month's good training.	
	4-8-18		Parade Service is held on the Battalion parade ground at 9.30am. 'D' Company produce a small choir, which is of considerable assistance in the singing. Immediately after parade a Regimental Court of Enquiry is held with Major B.K. COOKE, M.C. as president to enquire into the circumstances under which 2 prisoners escaped from the custody of the Quarter Guard on the night we left Aldershot to come overseas. During the afternoon the Commanding Officer is taken suddenly ill with an attack of fever. Two riding horses, which originally belonged to the 6th Bn. Oxford & Bucks Lt. Infty. and which were sent to the Transport Depôt at CUCQ when that Battalion was disbanded, are recovered, 2 of our new horses being given in exchange. Ten signallers are sent off to the Divisional Signal School for a course of instruction lasting about 5 weeks.	
	5-8-18		Training commenced. 6 hours work a day is done with as much boxing football & athletics as possible. As regards	

D. D. & L., London, E.C.
(A10266) W1 W5300/P713 750,000 2/18 Sch. 52 Forms/C2118/16.

WAR DIARY
~~or~~
~~INTELLIGENCE SUMMARY.~~

(*Erase heading not required.*)

Army Form C. 2118.

Instructions regarding War Diaries and Intelligence Summaries are contained in F. S. Regs., Part II. and the Staff Manual respectively. Title pages will be prepared in manuscript.

Place	Date	Hour	Summary of Events and Information	Remarks and references to Appendices
	5-8-18 (contd)		specialists, Signallers are all despatched to Division or Brigade for Courses of Instruction; Lewis Gunners do 3 hours specialist training during the morning under Company Instructors; Scouts the same under 2/Lt. H.VAUGHAN, the Battalion Scout Officer; instruction in Bombing is given to one company a day by Lieut. J.H.JACKSON; Stretcher bearers receive 2 hours training from the Medical Officer during the morning. During the afternoon all Specialists except the Signallers are with their companies for training. Under orders from the Brigade, training this week is to be progressive, 2 days being given to Section Training, 2 to Platoon, and 2 to Company Training. A class of about 20 junior N.C.O'S is formed under the Regtl. Sergt. Major, working 5½ hours a day. A lecture is given to the subaltern officers every evening by different Officers of the Battalion. Training grounds are quite good and conveniently situated. There are 2 miniature rifle ranges and one bombing ground in the village. The Battalion parade ground is a large expanse of grass land just outside the village; unfortunately the owner is always trying to plough part of it up and a good deal of trouble is caused. 2/Lts J.McKECHNIE & R.C.WHITE and all Signallers proceed to Bde. H.Q. for a Signalling Course.	
	6.8.18		Frequent showers rather interfere with training. Orders originally coming from G.H.Q are received to the effect that Infantry Battalions are temporarily to be organised on the 3 section to the platoon basis, each platoon having 2 rifle sections and one double Lewis Gun Section. The Battalion is reorganised on those lines forthwith. The Commanding Officer is considerably better today 2/Lt. J.S.DURANT is admitted to hospital today	
	7.8.18		Training is now in full swing, and the men appear to be coming on very well. The last of the inter-Company football games is played this evening; we can now see what talent we have, and can begin to choose the Battalion team.	
	8.8.18		A Battalion Sports Committee is formed under Major B.K.COOKE as president, with 2 Officers from the Battalion, the Regtl. Sgt. Major & 2 other ranks from each Company as members; arrangements are made for athletic training for the Brigade Sports to be held towards the end of the month. The Quarter Guard tonight found by 'C' Company is excellent the best we have had up to date. A&C Companies carry out night operations from 9.0 – 11.0 pm: all very successful, the work done by everyone being good.	
	9.8.18		The Transport is inspected by Major R.A.CLARKSON WEBB, A.S.C; the harness and general turn-out of the men is poor but the vehicles and the majority of the animals look quite well. B&D Companies carry out night operations; these are as successful as those of last night.	
	10.8.18		A Battalion boxing competition is held in the afternoon; about twenty men entered and the general style was extremely good, considerably above the average; it was especially noticeable for the good spirit of fair play which	

D. D. & L., London, E.C.
(A10266) Wt W5300/P713 750,000 2/18 Sch. 52 Forms/C2118/16.

Army Form C. 2118.

Instructions regarding War Diaries and Intelligence Summaries are contained in F. S. Regs., Part II. and the Staff Manual respectively. Title pages will be prepared in manuscript.

WAR DIARY
or
INTELLIGENCE SUMMARY.
(Erase heading not required.)

Place	Date	Hour	Summary of Events and Information	Remarks and references to Appendices
	10.8.18 (Contd)		prevailed in all the fights. At 6.30pm the Officers played the Sergeants at football and were beaten by 3 goals to one after an excellent game.	
	11.8.18		Church Parade is held at 9.30am. The singing is poor and not much help is given by the choir, who indeed broke down at the last hymn. Several enemy aeroplanes came over during the morning, probably to see what damage was done last night in Boulogne & Etaples by their bombing raid.	
	12.8.18		Orders have been received that 2 companies are to carry out firing practice tomorrow, on a range some 6 miles away; B&C Companies march out early to the neighbourhood of the range and bivouac there; the weather is perfect and the ground chosen for the camp excellent so that the whole operation was a success. A&D Companies carry out platoon training at HALINGHEN.	
	13.8.18		The shooting on the range was not very good owing to bad light principally. B&C Companies return about 9.0pm. Lieut. R.H. BEATTIE, 2/Lts. A.H. WARR, H.J. FARROW & A. ELLIS & 3 N.C.O's proceed to Le Touquet for the Lewis Gun course.	
	14.8.18		3 men are sent to the Divisional Signal Course at LONGUEREQUE for a 10 day course. The G.O.C. 1st Army, General HORNE, inspects the Division going round to each unit. The original order was that he would see us at training but at 2.30pm we are told that he will inspect us on parade; so the whole Battalion is hastily assembled, transport and employed personnel being of course left off. The General arrived about 4.30pm and made a hasty inspection of the men; the parade and march past were very successful, the drums being especially complimented. As a result of this inspection we are now regarded as an "A" Division. 'C' Company relieve 'D' at HAUT PICHOT during the evening; the latter are very sorry to go. Lieut. A. GORRINGE is admitted to hospital today suffering from an injury to his elbow.	
	15.8.18		Specialist training is now carried out in the afternoon only, so that Company Commanders have their full companies for 3 hours in the morning for manoeuvre and tactical exercises. In the evening the Commanding Officer gives a lecture to all Officers on the new system of training to be carried out in the British Forces under the direction of Lieut. General Maxse.	
	16.8.18		Lt. Col. Summers, the Divisional CRE comes into lunch today. 2/Lt. H.B. STRIDE joined the Battalion today.	
	17.8.18		Companies carry out 3 hours training in the morning; night operations are ordered for the evening, but these are prevented by rain. The Brigade Horse Show takes place today in an open field between HALINGHEN and TINGRY. Our successes are considerably	

D. D. & L., London, E.C.
(A10266) Wt W5300/P713 750,000 2/18 Sch. 52 Forms/C2118/16.

Instructions regarding War Diaries and Intelligence Summaries are contained in F. S. Regs., Part II. and the Staff Manual respectively. Title pages will be prepared in manuscript.

WAR DIARY
~~or~~
~~INTELLIGENCE SUMMARY.~~

(Erase heading not required.)

Army Form C. 2118.

Place	Date	Hour	Summary of Events and Information	Remarks and references to Appendices
	17-8-18 (Contd)		quicker than we had expected; 2/Lt T.E. COOKE, the Transport Officer, wins the infantry officers chargers event, our pair of heavy draught horses were the best, and we were a good second both in the limber driving competition and in the travelling kitchen event; in the last named our men alone of all the competitors had taken the trouble to clean themselves up. Unfortunately the weather broke towards the end of the afternoon and the parade of prize-winners & the presentation of prizes had to be cancelled.	
	18-8-18		Church Parade is held at 9.30am. and is altogether a more satisfactory business than previously. Capt. F.D. HEATH, Lieut E.F. SAXTON & 1 sergeant are sent to the First Army School at HARDELOT for a course of instruction; 2/Lt H. VAUGHAN and 1 L/Cpl. are sent to the 3rd. Army Lewis Gun School at FORT MAHON. Orders are received that the Division is to proceed to the forward area and take over part of the line this week. A party to reconnoitre the line to be taken over, consisting of the Commanding Officer, 2/Lt R.E. SMITH, the Intelligence Officer, and 1 Officer & 1 NCO per Company leave here in the evening for the 47th Inf. Bde H.Q with whom they will proceed to the line by bus tomorrow.	
	19.8.18		All arrangements are made for the move tomorrow. The transport, with all battalion baggage except our Lewis Guns and cooking utensils for Officers and men which will come with us by bus, moves off at 4.30 pm under orders of the 144th Company A.S.C. 2/Lt G.E. SANKEY is admitted to Hospital suffering from Hernia.	
	20.8.18		The Battalion, less transport, leaves HALINGHEN at 7.0am for the starting point on the SAMER - MONTREUIL road; embussment starts at 9.0am. and we finally move about 10.15 am. Our destination is the DIEVAL area where we are to stay the night; the route taken is through SAMER, DESVRES, THEROUANNE, ESTREE-BLANCHE, & CAMBRIN: our busses are very old and decrepit having been in use since 1914, but we all arrive eventually after several breaks-down about 5.30 p.m. & reach our billets in BOURS 1 hour late. Lieut G.C. PENSTONE & 1 NCO proceed to 1st. Army Musketry School MATRINGHEM.	
	21.8.18		At 11.0am. we leave BOURS and march to DIEVAL carrying our Lewis Guns and magazines. It is an oppressively hot day and the men are very much weighed down with all the kit to be carried. We embus again at DIEVAL and proceed from there about 1.45 pm to NOEUX LES MINES, passing through BRUAY, arriving at 3.45 p.m. There we find that owing to recent shelling no troops are allowed in the town, so we bivouac in the fields outside. Baths are arranged for the men and those who cannot bathe tonight will do so tomorrow morning. The forward party joins us again.	
	22.8.18		Some little shelling by H.V. guns rather interfere with the men's bathing, but no casualties are caused.	

D. D. & L., London, E.C.
(A10266) Wt W5300/P713 750,000 2/18 Sch. 52 Forms/C2118/16.

Instructions regarding War Diaries and Intelligence Summaries are contained in F. S. Regs., Part II. and the Staff Manual respectively. Title pages will be prepared in manuscript.

WAR DIARY
~~or~~
INTELLIGENCE SUMMARY.
(*Erase heading not required.*)

Army Form C. 2118.

Place	Date	Hour	Summary of Events and Information	Remarks and references to Appendices
	22.8.18 (contd)		The Battalion moves off by platoons at 300 yds. distance at 10.55 am. to relieve the 1st Bn. The [illegible] in the line. The sector lies immediately east of CAMBRIN, with its left on the LA BASSEE CANAL and its right on the CAMBRIN–LA BASSEE road; the length of front, as the crow flies being about 800 yds. It is held – with [illegible] a defensive flank on the left facing north across the canal – by 3 companies (D.B.A) in the front line, the right being somewhat refused, & 1 company (C) in support. The position is rather complicated by the presence of 3 small brick stacks in the centre front; these are held by small groups. The 2 front lines are some little distance apart, as both sides have withdrawn from their old front lines and the main line of resistance is now the original reserve line. The sector is a quiet one with luxurious trenches and dug-outs. Stores can be brought up by road & light railway to the trenches. It is a very hot day and the men though only wearing battle order are heavily loaded with Lewis Guns & stores; the front line is [illegible] miles from the starting point, & it is a great struggle for the men to go the distance. Relief is complete by 5.0 pm, very assistance having been given by the 1st [illegible]. A quiet night follows and all settle down very comfortably.	
	23.8.18		Another hot day. Everyone is very busy getting acquainted with the sector. The Commanding Officer has a conference of company commanders in the evening and gives them some instructions as to precautions which should be taken in the event of a British attack which is likely to take place shortly on our left. Capt. BLEEK an old Officer of the 5th Oxfords comes to tea.	
	24.8.18		The 55th Division on our left carry out a very successful minor operation at 7.20 am. resulting in the capture of the old [illegible] line. There is some slight shelling on our front and a little gas shelling but no casualties are caused. The Brigadier comes round the front line in the morning and stays to lunch afterwards. Lt. Col. F.D. BELLEW D.S.O., M.C. commanding the 6th Som. L.I. also lunches with us. Major Simpson, commanding a battery of R.F.A. of the 1st. Division now covering our front drops into mess in the evening. 2/Lt. C. ROSE proceeds to FRESSIN for a Gas course at the III Corps School.	
	26.8.18		The enemy counter attack about 4.30 am. on our left to regain the ground lost yesterday, but are not successful. Slight shelling on our front. Capt. T.E.G. McCARTHIE, M.C. the Divisional Gas Officer, Capt. T.W. McDONALD, D.S.O. & Lieut. BOND, M.C. our Brigade Major & Intelligence Officer come to tea.	

D. D. & L., London, E.C.
(A10266) Wt.W5300/P713 750,000 2/18 Sch. 52 Forms/C2118/16.

Army Form C. 2118.

Instructions regarding War Diaries and Intelligence Summaries are contained in F. S. Regs., Part II. and the Staff Manual respectively. Title pages will be prepared in manuscript.

WAR DIARY
~~or~~
~~INTELLIGENCE SUMMARY.~~

(Erase heading not required.)

Place	Date	Hour	Summary of Events and Information	Remarks and references to Appendices
	26-8-18		News is received that the house occupied by the Officers at the Transport Camp was hit by a shell at 10.30pm. last night and four of the French girls living there were killed. All our Officers, the 2nd in Command especially, had very narrow escapes. Very little important kit was destroyed except the despatch box containing the P.R.I. cheque books & documents, receipts etc. Some desultory shelling during the day from 5-9 & 4-5 hours & a little gas shelling; no casualties resulted from it. A soldier of 'B' Company is wounded, self-inflicted, in the left wrist	[illegible]
	27-8-18		'C' Company relieves 'A' in the left front sector during the afternoon; companies concerned make their own arrangements. B & D Companies carry out inter-platoon reliefs. A quiet day. 'B' Company has another accident. 2/Lt. STRIDE & his servant while visiting the platoon posts are mistaken for Germans; a bomb is thrown at them and the servant is killed immediately	[illegible]
	28-8-18		Capt. R.N. ADDINGTON proceeds on leave. Sgt POOK the Battalion Scout Sergeant takes out a small patrol to reconnoitre the ground and wire in front of the junction of B & C Companies; nothing of interest to report. Some shelling during the evening on MOUNTAIN KEEP and VILLAGE LINE; 1 slight casualty in 'A' Company.	[illegible]
	29-8-18		Another soldier of 'D' Company, wounded, self-inflicted, with a S.O.S. rifle. Major General A.B. RITCHIE, the Divisional Commander, the AA & QMG & GSO II visit the line in the afternoon. A Court of Enquiry is held to enquire into the circumstances under which Pte. RICHARDSON of B Company was killed on 27th inst. president Major COOKE, members Capt. STACE and Lt. JACKSON. 'B' Company send out a reconnaissance patrol in the neighbourhood of Argyle and Sutherland Sap at 10.0 pm; the patrol was out for 1½ hours and on return had nothing of particular interest to report. 2/Lt. T.H. HOLMES joins the Battalion today. Lt. BEATTIE & 2/Lts. FARROW & WARR with 8 NCO'S return from the G.H.Q. Lewis Gun Course.	[illegible]
	30.8.18		Reconnaissance of the trenches by O.C. 22nd. Northumberland Fusiliers who will relieve us tomorrow.	[illegible]
	31.8.18		Relieved by day-light. The Relief was completed easily, the only element of confusion being produced by the passing of the large un-notified working parties (one 6 p.m. [illegible] the other by the Pioneer Bn.) right through the trench system at the time the relief had been in progress about an hour. The Commanding Officer noticed the familiar mistake of Platoon Officers leading their Platoons out & allowing their heavily loaded Lewis Gun Sections to march last; thus making for lack of cohesion from the start. The Battalion took over bivouacs and billets in NOEUX-LES-MINES. Two Companies were able to get Baths today; the remainder will bathe tomorrow.	[illegible]

[illegible signature]
LT. COL.
CDG. 18th BN. GLOUCESTERSHIRE REGT.

D. D. & L., London, E.C.
(A10266) Wt W5300/P713 750,000 2/18 Sch. 52 Forms/C2118/16.

Instructions regarding War Diaries and Intelligence Summaries are contained in F. S. Regs, Part II. and the Staff Manual respectively. Title pages will be prepared in manuscript.

WAR DIARY
or
~~INTELLIGENCE SUMMARY.~~

(Erase heading not required.)

18 Gloucester Rg

Army Form C. 2118.

VIII 2

Place	Date	Hour	Summary of Events and Information	Remarks and references to Appendices
	1/9/18		Battalion moves from Bivouacs into Hutments recently vacated by Portuguese. Day is spent in generally cleaning up and completing the Bathing of the Batt[n]. Fritz pays considerable attention to the pit-heads and mine buildings in NOEUX-LES-MINES during the afternoon, and in the night enemy planes are continually hovering overhead but fail to distribute any bombs in the immediate vicinity of the camp	[illegible]
	2/9/18		Training begins and is carried out by Platoons under their own Commanders. 2/Lt HICKS platoon is sent on a working party at Div[l] Bomb Dump, BALLY BUNION. The latter part of the day was to have been spent in marching to the Range at REBREUVE, there to bivouac for the night. At midday, however, the weather conditions were such that the Colonel cancelled the parade. 2/Lieut STRIDE attends at Barlin as a member of a F.G.C.M. held on L/Cpl FRAZER of this Battalion. The Adjutant proceeds to England on leave, his place being temporarily filled by Lt. T.E. COOKE, who in turn is replaced by Lt A.H. BEATTIE as Transport Officer.	[illegible]
	3/9/18		The Battalion, less Transport and Specialists, marches out to REBREUVE for range practice under the supervision of CAPT KING. Weather is A1 and a very successful day is spent. After having dinners and tea out on range Batt[n] returns to Camp some after 6 p.m. Usual Specialist Training. R.S.M. TOPLIS evacuated as a result of his experiences on the night of the 25th and is succeeded by 2/Lt R.C. White (acting). CAPT G.C. WETHERALL rejoins from 18th Bde R.G.A.	[illegible]
	4/9/18		Platoons given to their Commanders for the morning. Our observation Balloon near transport lines attracts the attention of the Boche Gunners during the morning, resulting in a speedy evacuation of the lines for an hour or so. CAPT KING proceeds on attachment to "Heavies" for 6 days. Owing to the absence of the Colonel at a Conference at 49th Bde H.Q., proposed night operations postponed	[illegible]
	5/9/18		R.S.M.s parade on football field – arms drill quite good. Remainder of morning spent in lectures and demonstrations of patrolling. Lewis Gunners carry out range practice on GAVION RANGE – Shooting quite satisfactory. Sergeants challenge Officers at football in the afternoon and receive an unexpected reverse. 8–2.	

D. D. & L., London, E.C.
(A10266) Wt W5300/P713 750,000 2/18 Sch. 52 Forms/C2118/16.

Army Form C. 2118.

Instructions regarding War Diaries and Intelligence Summaries are contained in F. S. Regs., Part II. and the Staff Manual respectively. Title pages will be prepared in manuscript.

WAR DIARY
or
INTELLIGENCE SUMMARY.
(Erase heading not required.)

Place	Date	Hour	Summary of Events and Information	Remarks and references to Appendices
	5/9/18 Contd		Major BK COOKE MC proceeds to UK on leave and is succeeded as 2nd in Command by CAPT GC WETHERALL. LT JACKSON proceeds to 1st Corps Staff on attachment. LT A CORRINGE returns from Hospital. The Battn parades for night operations at 8-30 PM and proceeds across country to position of assembly in case of enemy attack. Operation carried out very well by all ranks. During our absence NOEUX-LES-MINES is treated to a heavy bombardment by HV guns; only two shells, however, fell near the Cantonments, remainder all near the mines.	[illegible]
	6/9/18		2 am sees the Battn back in Camp from night operations. Tea served to men, none of whom have fallen out despite having covered about 7 miles. Reveille not until 9 am. Inspection of S.B.Rs is the only parade. At 1-30 pm Battn starts out, headed by band, to visit the BLACKTHORNS at BARLIN, but are recalled by orders to take over defence of CAMBRIN locality from 6th [illegible] L.I., which is accomplished rapidly and smoothly. Bn HQ arriving in CAMBRIN [illegible] [illegible] the [illegible] [illegible] 9 pm. Companies scattered all over the village in cellars, but are fairly comfortable and a quiet night is spent.	[illegible]
	7/9/18		Very quiet day. Brig Gen Bray DSO [illegible] 18 Inf Bde visits Bn HQ during conference of Coy Commanders and afterwards sees B Coy demonstrate an advance by [illegible]. Bn Companies bathe and get clean clothes. Coy Commanders reconnoitre left [illegible] Sector prior to taking over on the morrow. CO and Adjt visit 22nd Northumberland Fusiliers' Bn HQrs and make arrangements for the relief.	[illegible]
	8/9/18		The Battalion prepares to move into the line shortly after 11 am, but relief is postponed by Brigade until 2 pm, at which time Companies commence to move. Miserable day and nobody looks or feels very happy. Relief not completed until nearly midnight when Companies are disposed as follows:- C Coy left front with posts just E of the [illegible] and along BRICKBAT ALLEY, Coy HQrs being at HASTINGS. D Coy right front on the line of AUBURN TRENCH, by no means a pleasant or comfortable locality, with Coy HQ [illegible] the Eastern End of the tunnel. A and B are left and right Support Companies, having their Company Headqrs at MARYLEBONE and [illegible] TUNNEL. Rations are brought up to NORTH DUMP on pack [illegible]	

D. D. & L., London, E.C.
(A10266) Wt W5300/P713 750,000 2/18 Sch. 52 Forms/C2118/16.

Instructions regarding War Diaries and Intelligence Summaries are contained in F. S. Regs., Part II. and the Staff Manual respectively. Title pages will be prepared in manuscript.

WAR DIARY
or
~~INTELLIGENCE SUMMARY.~~

(Erase heading not required.)

Army Form C. 2118.

Place	Date	Hour	Summary of Events and Information	Remarks and references to Appendices
	7/9/18 contd.		notes. [illegible] on to the forward Companies by parties from the supports	
	9/9/18		Orders are received from 14th Inf Bde for the Battn to attack on the morning of [illegible] in conjunction with the [illegible] with the following as objectives – RAILWAY TRIANGLE, SPOTTED DOG and RAILWAY COTTAGE [illegible] by bounds and [illegible] with no artillery barrage. After [illegible] with the Coy Commanders the CO decides that attack shall be carried out by the companies now in line, [illegible] C and D Coys and [illegible] remaining in support, and orders are issued accordingly (see Operation Order No 12). Battalion HQ [illegible] now in [illegible] a small and exceedingly uncomfortable dug-out in MARLBORNE, are [illegible] with representatives of various branches of the service, all directly or indirectly interested in the forthcoming minor operation, including the CRA, [illegible] Artillery Group, OC Heavies, [illegible] TMB, [illegible] TMBs, OC 157 Field Coy RE, 170th Tunnelling Coy RE and many others. Everything is at last finally arranged just before midnight, when orders are received from 14th Inf Bde that operations are postponed for 24 hours.	//
	10/9/18		Brig Gen [illegible] Commdg 14th Inf Bde is early on the scene and the morning is spent in a conference which is attended by the Coy Commanders, the G.S.O. apparently wishing to satisfy himself that Coy Commanders know their job. As yesterday a [illegible] of [illegible] [illegible] Battn HQ all day long, and during the day the heavy Trench Mortars and Hows give the wire in front of SPOTTED DOG and the STATION a little attention, but the result of their fire cannot be observed. Operation Order No 13 are issued and reconnaissance patrols are sent out along the whole front to be attacked. Fairly quiet night. Zero has been fixed at 5.15 am.	//
	11/9/18		At Zero artillery of both sides is fairly active, but not unusually so. C and D Companies, having pushed as close as possible to their objectives under cover of darkness, have [illegible] trouble and practically no opposition in gaining the desired ground and commence to consolidate the positions won. Four prisoners, including an under officer, together with a machine gun are secured by D Coy in	

D. D. & L., London, E.C.
(A10266) Wt W5300/P713 750,000 2/18 Sch. 52 Forms/C2118/16.

Instructions regarding War Diaries and Intelligence Summaries are contained in F. S. Regs., Part II. and the Staff Manual respectively. Title pages will be prepared in manuscript.

WAR DIARY
or
~~INTELLIGENCE SUMMARY.~~

(Erase heading not required.)

Army Form C. 2118.

Place	Date	Hour	Summary of Events and Information	Remarks and references to Appendices
	11/9/18		front of SPOTTED DOG. Apparently the work of consolidation had been in progress some time when the enemy counter attacked, emerging with [illegible] from cellars and dugouts in the neighbourhood of TURNTABLE ALLEY and SPOTTED DOG and succeeded in regaining possession of the latter. This rendered the holding of TURNTABLE ALLEY and the STATION impracticable and O.C. Coys accordingly ordered the evacuation of these positions. At 11 am therefore the Battn was back on the line reached prior to the attack. Casualties in this action: 2nd Lieuts WARR and GRAY wounded, other ranks – 9 killed, 19 wounded 1 missing.	
			Orders are received shortly after 2 pm for the attack to be repeated at 5.45 pm. Company Commanders are summoned to Battn HQ and verbal orders are issued. Owing to poor communications some platoons are warned only a few minutes prior to the attack. At 5.45 our artillery (Heavies included) and a terrific barrage falls on the objectives, the shooting on the Station and SPOTTED DOG being particularly effective. Punctually at 5.45 pm the barrage lifts and our men can be seen advancing in [illegible] movement apparently with little opposition. It is 6 minutes after Zero when the first [illegible] shell falls in our lines, but by this time our troops are well past the enemy S.O.S. line. The coveted positions are taken with ease and prisoners to the number of 23, in addition to 5 machine guns all belonging to the 369th I.R. 10th Ersatz Division fall into our hands. Anticipated counter attacks fail to materialise and the work of consolidation proceeds unhindered, save for desultory shelling which does little or no damage. Our casualties on this occasion amount to: Capt Stace and Lt Elliott wounded. O.R. – 12 killed 23 wounded 1 missing.	JH
	12/9/18		Work of consolidation proceeding entirely without interference on the part of Fritz who seems to have been caught napping and is apparently still disorganised. Men are [illegible] but quite cheerful and all anxious to explore AUCHY which looks very tempting from a souvenir hunter's point of view. An officer's patrol led by 2/Lt FULLER reveals the fact that the village is not	

D. D. & L., London, E.C.
(A10266) Wt W5300/P713 750,000 2/18 Sch. 52 Forms/C2118/16.

Instructions regarding War Diaries and Intelligence Summaries are contained in F. S. Regs., Part II. and the Staff Manual respectively. Title pages will be prepared in manuscript.

WAR DIARY
or
~~INTELLIGENCE SUMMARY.~~
(Erase heading not required.)

Army Form C. 2118.

Place	Date	Hour	Summary of Events and Information	Remarks and references to Appendices
	12/9/18		occupied except by a singularly dejected young woman of some 18 years, very tired, frightened and hungry, who is escorted to the rear. An extraordinarily uneventful day passes during which large parties of [illegible] go through the neighbourhood recently occupied by the enemy, seemingly under direct observation from their lines. The Battalion is relieved during the evening by the 23rd Northumberland Fusiliers and goes into support in the VILLAGE and Reserve line. All ranks exceedingly tired but an issue of rum awakens their interest in life for a few minutes after which any traces of life in the area occupied are few and far between.	[illegible]
	13/9/18		As a precautionary measure, fresh socks and whale oil are issued out to the men, but several cases of trench feet are reported, no doubt owing to the muddy state of the ground occupied [illegible]. Companies are busy reorganising and cleaning up and parties are sent out to bring back our captured machine guns as well as some of the many Lewis Gun Drums lying about in the forward area. During the day Fritz pays particular attention to the crossroads and other conspicuous points in the locality, but leaves us quite alone. 2/Lt HILL evacuated suffering with trench feet. Lt GORRINGE arrives from Transport Camp and assumes Command of A Company.	[illegible]
	14/9/18		Large salvage parties are sent out by Companies and a considerable quantity of valuable material is recovered, two truck loads being sent to the Div. Salvage Dump. Very quiet day. Two platoons of B Coy carry for Northumberland Fusiliers during the evening. Capt ADDINGTON returns from leave and Lt PENSTONE from a Course.	[illegible]
	15/9/18		Activities of the Battalion again chiefly confined to Salvage work and a further quantity of serviceable material is collected and sent down to the Dump. Another exceedingly quiet and peaceful day. A Coy find 2 carrying parties in the evening. Fritz distributes a few gas shells along the reserve line but beyond causing A Coy a little annoyance does no damage.	[illegible]

D. D. & L., London, E.C.
(A10266) Wt W5300/P713 750,000 2/18 Sch. 52 Forms/C2118/16.

Instructions regarding War Diaries and Intelligence Summaries are contained in F. S. Regs., Part II. and the Staff Manual respectively. Title pages will be prepared in manuscript.

WAR DIARY
or
INTELLIGENCE SUMMARY.
(Erase heading not required.)

Army Form C. 2118.

Place	Date	Hour	Summary of Events and Information	Remarks and references to Appendices
	16/9/18		Yet another quiet day. Enemy aircraft fairly active overhead but don't trouble us at all and are too high for us to trouble them. Company Commanders reconnoitre the positions of the 22nd Northumberland Fusiliers preparatory to taking over tomorrow. C Coy find two platoons to carry for NFs.	[illegible]
	17/9/18		Yet another quiet morning. The Commanding Officer holds a conference of Company Commanders prior to relieving the 22nd Northumberland Fusiliers. At 4 pm however, the NFs are counter attacked in their new positions immediately South of the LA BASSEE CANAL and their forward posts are driven back. The relief however is proceeded with and B C & D Companies report their relief complete by 10 pm. One Company of the NFs again attacks at 1 am to regain the lost posts. The attack is successful and A Company which is now under the Command of Lt A GORRINGE reports having relieved the front Company at 2 am on the morning of the 18th.	[illegible]
	18/9/18		The night passes quietly and the morning is spent in settling down in our new positions. Major MONK (the GSO 2) visits the Battn and proceeds round the line. After a short bombardment, however, the left front posts are again attacked by the Boches and our posts are driven back having 20 casualties. Preparation is at once made to counter attack, but the GSO 2 who returns from the line agrees with the Commanding Officer, and later, Brigade orders the counter attack not to be made. Lt TE COOKE the Acting Adjutant proceeds to the U.K. on leave and the Adjutant, CAPT SL SYMONDS MC returns to duty after a well merited rest.	[illegible]
	19/9/18		No particular activity on the part of the enemy. A little machine gun fire and some desultory shelling of the forward area; an unlucky shell knocks out a Lewis Gun team of A Company, otherwise no damage is done. A thorough search is made for any wounded men who might have been left lying out in front, but none are found. 3 Lewis Gun teams from the Cyclist Corps are attached to us, 2 to A Company and 1 to D and prove very useful. Every effort made to strengthen and consolidate our positions, the men, though tired, work very well.	[illegible]
	20/9/18		Some shelling of the left front posts about 9.0 am otherwise little enemy activity. Warning order received that our Divisional Front will probably be shortened. The 5th Division on our	

D. D. & L., London, E.C.
(A10266) Wt W5300/P713 750,000 2/18 Sch. 52 Forms/C2118/16.

Instructions regarding War Diaries and Intelligence Summaries are contained in F. S. Regs., Part II. and the Staff Manual respectively. Title pages will be prepared in manuscript.

WAR DIARY
or
~~INTELLIGENCE SUMMARY.~~
(*Erase heading not required.*)

Army Form C. 2118.

Place	Date	Hour	Summary of Events and Information	Remarks and references to Appendices
	20/9/18 Contd		left will take over to the La Bassee Road and the 15th on our right take over another portion; our front will then be held by 1 Brigade only. At midnight a fighting patrol of 1 Officer and 5 men is sent out to reconnoitre the DISTILLERY, a building some 600 yards to our front. This patrol is preceded by a reconnoitring patrol of 1 Serjeant and 7 men who are to go out and make good part of the Ground. This first patrol however is held up some 250 yards in front of our wire by machine gun fire, and neither party can get forward. Some useful information is obtained as to the location of enemy machine guns, which is given to the Artillery, and as a result good shooting is made on the guns in question. Early in the morning 1 Lance Corporal (No 21711 L/Cpl MOULDING W.H and six men of A Company who were holding the left front post on the 18th last and were believed to have been captured come back into our lines, having remained at their posts all the time unmolested save for shelling. A very stout hearted performance.	
	21/9/18		Some shelling of CAMBRIN and MOUNTAIN KEEP during the early morning, otherwise the day is quiet. Orders received that we are to be relieved by a Battalion of the 56th Division. Officers of the relieving unit come up during the morning to arrange the particulars. They are to take over with 2 Companies, one holding the forward area and one in support. Brig Gen BRAY interviews the L/Cpl and 6 men of A Company who held out in the front post, and compliments them on their good work. The relieving Companies start moving in from across the Canal about 6.0 pm and relief is complete about 9.45 pm. On relief the Battalion passes into reserve, HQ and 2 Companies (A+D) being in CAMBRIN, B in village line and C in the continuation of that trench South of the LA BASSEE ROAD. All Companies are in position by 11.0 pm. Total Casualties in the last four days are 4 killed 20 wounded and 5 missing. Major B.K. COOKE M.C. returns from leave.	

D. D. & L., London, E.C.
(A10266) Wt W5300/P713 750,000 2/18 Sch. 52 Forms/C2118/16.

Army Form C. 2118.

WAR DIARY
or
~~INTELLIGENCE SUMMARY.~~
(Erase heading not required.)

Instructions regarding War Diaries and Intelligence Summaries are contained in F. S. Regs., Part II. and the Staff Manual respectively. Title pages will be prepared in manuscript.

Place	Date	Hour	Summary of Events and Information	Remarks and references to Appendices
	22/9/18		A draft of 128 Other Ranks arrives at the Divisional Reception Camp for the Battn. Companies are settled in pretty comfortably though the positions occupied by B.&C. are rather dangerous, being immediately in ~~front~~ front of the batteries and in consequence heavily shelled. Orders are received late at night for C. Company to move into posts some 400 yards of their left, their positions being taken by a company of the Royal Irish Rifles.	
	23/9/18		115 Other Ranks of the Draft arrive, the remainder being kept at the Reception Camp for training as Specialists. All are private soldiers except 2 and belong to Category B1, the majority coming from Lancashire and being transferred to us from the R.W.F. They are divided ~~up~~ equally among the Companies. 2nd Lieut C.A. BRAMELD rejoins from 1st Corps Course. Capt D.L. JACKS M.C. is admitted to hospital	
	24/9/18		Baths at ANNEQUIN are allotted to the Battalion today and every man gets a bath and a change of clothing. The whole draft that arrived yesterday is sent back to the Reception Camp as being not physically fit for trench life; more than one of them are men who were 'cast' from the Battn in England. At 6.0.pm. the Battalion moves up into support, relieving the 6th Somerset L.I.; relief is completed about 8.30. pm.	
	25/9/18		Some shelling of MOUNTAIN KEEP and VILLAGE line by 5.9 in the morning and again by gas shells at night; otherwise a very quiet day. Brig Gen HORDERN, B.G.C.S. 1st Corps visits the Battalion about 10. pm. and goes on to see RAILWAY TRIANGLE. A working party of 2 platoons provided for R.E.	
	26/9/18		Fine weather continues. Arrangements made with 22nd Northumberland Fusiliers for relief tomorrow.	
	27/9/18		Quiet day. The 49th Brigade is relieved by the 48th and the battalion goes out to ANNEQUIN, H.Qrs and 3 Companies being there, the 4th being in the village line. Relief is complete at 5.45 pm	

D. D. & L., London, E.C.
(A10266) Wt W5300/P713 750,000 2/18 Sch. 52 Forms/C2118/16.

Instructions regarding War Diaries and Intelligence Summaries are contained in F. S. Regs., Part II. and the Staff Manual respectively. Title pages will be prepared in manuscript.

WAR DIARY
or
~~INTELLIGENCE SUMMARY.~~

(Erase heading not required.)

Army Form C. 2118.

Place	Date	Hour	Summary of Events and Information	Remarks and references to Appendices
	27/9/18 Contd.		and everyone settles in fairly comfortably for the night	
			CAPT F HEATH and LIEUT EF SAXTON returns from 1st Army Course	
	28/9/18		CAPT JA STACE rejoins from hospital. Baths at [illegible] again allotted to the Battalion. Two companies are detailed for work under the RE and Pioneer battalion, 2 Platoons starting at 8.0 am and the remainder at various hours in the evening from 7 pm to 10.30 pm. Another draft of 5? all category men arrive at the Reception Camp. The first draft of 125 were medically examined today and roughly 40% were found unfit	
	29/9/18		Working parties found as yesterday. All training possible is carried out, special attention being paid to individual training and general endeavour to brighten the men up.	
	30/9/18		FGCM assembles on Pte LLEWLLYN of C Company who is tried on a charge of misbehaving in such a manner as to show cowardice and of desertion. A Company relieves D in MILLAIS LINE. The first platoon of A moves off at 4.30 pm and relief is complete by 6.0 pm. Miserable wet day	

[signature]
LT. COL.
CDG. 18th BN. GLOUCESTERSHIRE REGT.

D. D. & L., London, E.C.
(A10266) Wt W5300/P713 750,000 2/18 Sch. 52 Forms/C2118/16.

S E C R E T Copy No......

18th. Bn. The Gloucestershire Regiment

OPERATION ORDER No.13. 10-9-1918.

Reference 49th. Inf. Bde. Order No. 27.
Map Reference Sheet 44A. N.W. 1
Intelligence Map No. 9.

1. The Battalion in conjunction with 6 SOM. L.I. on the right will advance on the morning of 11. 9. 18. and occupy a line of posts as follows :-

18th. Gloucesters - (i) Trench junction A.22.b.75.40.
(ii) SPOTTED DOG (including) A.22.b.6.6.
(iii) Trench junctions about A.22.b.8.7.
(iv) TURNTABLE ALLEY about A.23.a.2.9.
(v) Railway Embankment at A.17.c.4.3.

2. The Right Battalion, 6 SOM.L.I. has been ordered to occupy RAILWAY COTTAGE A.22.d.4.8. and line of Railway through A.22.c.and & bifurcation at A.22.c.90.00. all inclusive.

3. "D" & "C" Companies will carry out the operations. A Platoon of "B" Company is attached to "D" and one of "A" to "C" as local Reserve. To "D" Company is allotted the first 3 objectives named in para 1 ; to "C" Company the last two.

4. Until further orders it is to be distinctly understood that AUBURN TRENCH remains the LINE OF RESISTANCE. "B" and "A" Coys (each less 1 Platoon) will occupy this Trench when the Battle Platoons found by the forward Companies have moved out.

5. ARTILLERY

(i) There will be no preliminary bombardment.

(ii) Wire cutting may be expected to-day - Hours will be notified to all concerned when information is received.

(iii) The following is quoted from 49th. Inf. Bde.No.B.O.27/1 dated 9. 9. 18.

"It has been arranged that, should the enemy during the operations shell the new line of Points, a Protective Barrage will be at once put down by Heavies, Field Artillery and Machine Guns.

This shelling by the enemy may be merely the shelling of the Post Line, or may be immediately prior to a counter-attack.

This will not in any way interfere with the Barrage put down in response to a S.O.S."

6. 2 Stokes Mortars will be in position by Zero - 2 at A.22.b.15.80 A.22.b.20.85. and will be available to assist the operations.

7. Zero hour is fixed at 5.15.a.m. Watches will be synchronized at 9. 0.p.m. to-night.

8. Role of the Forward Companies.

(i) Careful reconnaissance by Patrol will be maintained during the night. It must be realized that the roite ultimately to be followed by the Battle Platoons, or the way out of the present outpost line, must depend upon the reconnaissance.

(Continued)

8. (Continued)

(ii) During the night Officers Commanding 'D' and 'C' Companies will advance such of their posts as they deem necessary to cover the further advance of the line.

They will not move any exixting post which already fulfills that function.

(iii) The Garrison of the Trench running from the CANAL to the N.E. corner of the DOCK will not be moved until the RAILWAY TRIANGLE has been made good. During the operations its function is to afford Covering Fire, if required, for the Battle Platoons detailed to infiltrate and turn the RAILWAY TRIANGLE locality from the SOUTH. If subsequently moved, its place will be taken by a Platoon found from the Supporting ("A") Company; the route to be selected by Officer Commanding "C" Company and Guides placed at the disposal of "A" Company for that purpose should the occasion arise.

(iv) The advance will be by Bounds i.e. a Line of Posts (the precise position of which must be determined by reconnaissance and modified by circumstances) must be established along the line A.22.b.22.10. - A.22.b.55.30.- A.22.b.25.50. - A.22.b.65.65.- A.22.b.85.80.- through which the Battle Platoons respectively detailed to capture SPOTTED DOG and to turn the RAILWAY TRIANGLE Defences will pass.

(v) Final Objectives :-

RIGHTVCOMPANY SPOTTED DOG with a post forward at trench junction A.22.b.85.40. The whole area to be carefully consolidated.

LEFT COMPANY The whole of the RAILWAY TRIANGLE locality bounded by the co-ordinates A.16.d.90.35.- A.17.c.40.35.- A.22.b.90.70.

9. CO-OPERATION.

(i) Co-operation must be intimate between Companies and between the Right of "D" Company and the troops found by 6 SOM.L.I.

(ii) The 2 first named posts in Para 8 sub.para (iv) are designated to form a defensive flank pending the capture and consolidating of RAILWAY COTTAGE by the Right Battalion. They may be withdrawn reinforced or pushed forward at the discretion of the Commander on the spot when they have fulfilled the primary role assigned them.

(iii) Movement against the primary objectives will be simultaneous at Zero Hour. The Left Company will not however commit itself toa penetration into the North Eastern part of the RAILWAY TRIANGLE until it is sure that SPOTTED DOG has been occupied or that the Right Flank of its Battle Platoon is otherwise protected and in touch with 'D' Coy.

10. In framing their own detailed orders, Officers Commanding Companies will be guided by the following instructions as to their use of Troops :-

(i) Reconnaissance Patrols will be found by Platoons now in front line system.

(ii) As far as possible the existing posts will be pushed forward to fulfil the conditions of para 8 sub para (ii).

(iii) Battle Platoons will be chosen from the Supports; and Reserve Platoons will be used boldly where stiffening is required or intensive consolidating is necessary.

(iv) Officers Commanding "A" and "B" Companies will without further orders maintain existing strength of Garrisons in AUBURN TRENCH. They may meet requests for reinforcements from Officers Commanding "C" & "D" Companies up to 1 Platoon each Company respectively. The remainder will not move without reference to Battalion Headquarters.

11. 22nd. Northumberland Fus. has been ordered to occupy MARYLEBONE with one Company at 4. a.m.

(Continued)

12. 2 Battalion Orderlies & 2 Signallers are attached to the forward Companies. Messages to indicate positions to Higher Authority will be sent by pigeons ; to Battalion Headquarters by Orderly.

13. Reports to Brickstacks (A.21.b.9.9.) from Z - 30 minutes. Should Battalion Headquarters move from there, its position will be notified to all concerned.

14. Administrative Orders will be issued at 5. P.M. to-day.

T.E.Cooke. Lieut & Act/Adjt.
18th. Bn. Gloucester Regiment.

DISTRIBUTION (issued at 3.35.p.m.)

Copy	1 - 4	Companies
"	5	6 SOM.L.I.
"	6	1/4th. N. LAN. R.
"	7	22nd. Northumberland Fus.
"	8	"C" Company. 16th. M.G.B.
"	9	49th. Inf. Bde.
"	10	File.

18th Gloucester Regt. 49/16

Oct 1918

Army Form C. 2118.

Instructions regarding War Diaries and Intelligence Summaries are contained in F. S. Regs., Part II. and the Staff Manual respectively. Title pages will be prepared in manuscript.

WAR DIARY
or
~~INTELLIGENCE~~ SUMMARY.

(*Erase heading not required.*)

Vol 3

Place	Date	Hour	Summary of Events and Information	Remarks and references to Appendices
	1.10.18		2/Lieut. R. HILL rejoins at the Divisional Reception Camp from hospital. 2 men are sent on a Signalling Course at Divisional Signal School at DROUVIN. Working parties are found as usual. Two men are sent to the First Army Rest Camp. 2/Lieut. H.W. VAUGHAN goes on leave. Riding class for Officers held in the afternoon.	
	2.10.18		Orders are received that we are to relieve the 34th London Regt in NOEUX-LES-MINES tomorrow, and all arrangements are made. These orders are cancelled at 6.0pm owing to a report from the R.A.F. that the Germans have retired beyond the HAUTE DEULE Canal. At 8.0pm we are ordered to be prepared to move at 3 hours notice. Riding class as usual.	
	3.10.18		Working parties are found as usual. At 11.0am orders are received that we are to relieve the Londons tomorrow but these are cancelled soon afternoon, and we are to stay here. The Londons coming through us to the VILLAGE LINE, and the Somersets moving up to SAILLY LABOURSE. Baths are allotted to the Battalion in the afternoon.	
	4.10.18		2/Lieut. W.A. KERSLAKE joins for duty and is posted to 'B' Company. 2/Lieut. HODGES rejoins from hospital. 2/Lts. SMITH and TOMS and 10 other ranks proceed to I Corps School HERLY. Working parties are no longer found, and all available time is devoted to training, a miniature range in the village is used for rifle and revolver shooting and 2 companies carry out training in intensive digging and wiring. Our front line is now at the HAUTE DEULE CANAL. Lt. Col. D.B. PARRY, D.S.O. Commanding the Divisional M.G. Battalion lunches with us today.	
	5.10.18		Training continued as yesterday. Riding class held again today.	
	6.10.18		Lieut. T.E. COOKE returns from leave. Church parade held in the courtyard of the Mine at 10.0am.	
	7.10.18		Training continued on the same lines as last week. All companies engaged during the morning in digging platoon posts. All the draft which has been waiting at the Reception Camp comes up today and is posted to companies. Arrangements made for relief by 9th Black Watch tomorrow.	
	8.10.18		2/Lt. G. ELAVEN-COOK reports for duty and is posted to 'C' Company. The Battalion is relieved at	

D. D. & L., London, E.C.
(A10266) Wt W5300/P713 750,000 2/18 Sch. 52 Forms/C2118/16.

Army Form C. 2118.

Instructions regarding War Diaries and Intelligence Summaries are contained in F. S. Regs., Part II. and the Staff Manual respectively. Title pages will be prepared in manuscript.

WAR DIARY
or
INTELLIGENCE SUMMARY.
(Erase heading not required.)

Place	Date	Hour	Summary of Events and Information	Remarks and references to Appendices
	8.10.18	(Contd)	13.15 and marches out to HESDIGNEUL, arriving at 16.30. Accomodation on the whole is excellent, the men being billetted in aeroplane hangars which unfortunately are rather cold. Parade and training grounds and range are very good and conveniently situated.	
	9.10.18		An hour's Battalion drill is carried out in the morning. Otherwise the day is devoted to administration, fitting new clothing, pay, etc.	
	10.10.18		A draft of 30 other ranks is received, all category B1 men. Training is begun in earnest, ½ of an hour Battalion drill to start with, followed by Platoon exercises for the remainder of the morning. 2 companies are on the range in the afternoon; the shooting is not very good. A class of from 4 to 6 young NCO's per Company assemble under the RSM and work from 14.00 to 16.00. In the evening the Commanding Officer gives a lecture to Subaltern Officers. Major Parish APM I Corps takes lunch with us. Capt. G.C. WETHERALL proceeds on leave; Capt. R.N. ADDINGTON, M.C. takes over 'D' Company.	
	11.10.18		Capt. O.L. JACKS, M.C. rejoins from hospital. Training carried out as for yesterday, special attention being paid to Ceremonial Drill: a great improvement is shown on the first battalion parade we had, and the men really work remarkably well, considering everything.	
	12.10.18		The Brigade is inspected by GOC Division at 10.00 near DROUVIN; medal ribbons are given away to those Officers, NCO'S and men who gained distinction in the recent fighting. Our Battalion easily heads the list in numbers of honours gained of the Brigade and even of the Division. The [illegible] to take the salute of the Brigade at the march past. In the evening the Battalion concert party gives its first show. Success was assured from the very start and the whole performance went with an extraordinary swing and delighted the whole audience. 2/Lt. A. FULLER who runs the party is to be heartily congratulated on the result of his work.	
	13.10.18		Church Parade is held in the Church Army Hut. In the afternoon officers played the sergeants and 'A' played 'D' Company at footer, the officers won easily in a very one-sided match. At 20.00 the Divisional Concert Party, 'The Blackthorns', gave a show in the Canteen; the whole Battalion managed to squeeze in, and gave an enthusiastic welcome to a really first class performance.	

D. D. & L., London, E.C.
(A10266) Wt W5300/P713 750,000 2/18 Sch. 52 Forms/C2118/16.

Instructions regarding War Diaries and Intelligence Summaries are contained in F. S. Regs., Part II. and the Staff Manual respectively. Title pages will be prepared in manuscript.

WAR DIARY
~~or~~
~~INTELLIGENCE~~ SUMMARY.
(*Erase heading not required.*)

Army Form C. 2118.

Place	Date	Hour	Summary of Events and Information	Remarks and references to Appendices
	14.10.18		At 09.15 the Battalion is inspected by B.G.C. and afterwards marches past in review order. In the afternoon a boxing competition is held, with great success, all the fights being very sportsmanlike and clean, though there was not quite so much good boxing as at the previous competition held at HALINGHEM. Tonight is a guest night at the Officers' Mess. The B.G.C., Capt. W.H. STITT, Staff Captain, Major GRANT, M.S.B. and 3 other officers are guests of the mess.	
	15.10.18		Two companies firing on the range in the morning and 2 in the afternoon. The shooting on the whole is poor. 2/Lt. ELLIOTT, M.C. returns from hospital. A draft of 73 O.R. arrives, apparently a very good lot.	
	16.10.18		One hour's Battalion drill in the morning, followed by advance guard exercise carried out by companies. In the evening the Sergeants entertain the Officers at a smoking concert; a merry evening is the result.	
	17.11.18		2/Lieut. H. VAUGHAN returns from leave. The Battalion moves to SAILLY LABOURSE via VAUDRICOURT and VERQUIGNEUL at 14.00 arriving in billets at 17.15. Blankets are taken on a lorry, but with this exception we depend entirely on the first line transport to move the stores; this of course has necessitated large quantities of stores being dumped at the Divisional Dump at SAILLY LABOURSE. Distance covered in the day is 8 miles. A warning order that we are to move forward again tomorrow is received about 18.30. Definite orders for the move arrive at 23.30	
	18.10.18		The Battalion moves forward at 09.00 accompanied by the transport to AUCHY. While on the way we receive orders to go right through to BAUVIN, if the line advances as expected. We have dinner at AUCHY and start again at 13.30, travelling through HAISNES and BERCLAU and arrive at 16.45, a most interesting march; the men got along very well considering everything, only 12 falling out. Distance covered in the day is 11 miles.	
	19.10.18		Orders to move to AVELIN are received at 03.45. The Battalion gets away at 09.10, marching via PROVIN - CARVIN - CAMPHIN - PALEMPHIN - ATTICHES; Dinner and tea are served on the road, and the Battalion gets in about 18.00; 20 men falling out, but all except 4 trudging in at the tail of the Bn.; the length of the march is roughly 14 miles. Billets are most comfortable, far the best ever occupied by this Battalion.	
	20.10.18		Orders to move to ENNEVELIN are received at 02.00. The Battalion moves at 09.00 and reaches the destination about 10.45, accomodation good. At 14.00 we get a warning order to move this afternoon. At 18.00 we	

D. D. & L., London, E.C.
(A10266) Wt W5300/P713 750,000 2/18 Sch. 52 Forms/C2118/16.

Instructions regarding War Diaries and Intelligence Summaries are contained in F. S. Regs., Part II. and the Staff Manual respectively. Title pages will be prepared in manuscript.

WAR DIARY

~~or~~

~~INTELLIGENCE~~ SUMMARY.

(Erase heading not required.)

Army Form C. 2118.

Place	Date	Hour	Summary of Events and Information	Remarks and references to Appendices
	20.10.18 (Contd)		move out again and march to HARDINIERE via HELIN and TEMPLEUVE; accomodation is very poor and insufficient and the men are not packed in till 21.00. No one fell out on the march, the distance covered was 8 miles.	
	21.10.18		Orders received to move to BACHY at 01.00. The Battalion moves at 10.20 arriving at 12.15, having marched through GENECH and LAPOSTERIE. Accomodation very fair. Distance covered during the day 5 miles. 2/Lieut J.S. DURANT rejoins from hospital.	
	22.10.18		A warning order is received to move today, but this is cancelled early in the morning. Everybody has a much needed rest all day. Arrangements are made for all the men to get baths, and this is done. Lieut. E.G. PENSTONE proceeds on leave.	
	23.10.18		2 companies are required at short notice for working parties, filling in craters on road etc. Lt. Col. PARRY, Comdg 16th Machine Gun Bn. takes lunch with us.	
	24.10.18		2/Lieut. R.E. SMITH rejoins from I Corps Course. 2/Lieut. R.W. MANTLE joins the Battalion. In the morning a tactical exercise in skeleton is carried out by all Officers, the signallers and stretcher bearers. In the evening the Battalion Concert Party gives 2 performances half the Bn. attending at each; in spite of the fact that they were without their box of properties and had almost nothing to make up with, a first class show was produced. Orders are received at 17.00 that the Brigade will relieve the forward Brigade tomorrow.	
	25.10.18		The Battalion moves at 10.00 relieving the 11th Leicester Regt. as Battalion in Reserve; H.Qs are at FLORE IT. 2 companies at TAINTEGNIES and 2 at LE PREAU. Dinner is served on the road and everyone is in quarters by 14.00 the accomodation being very fair on the whole. Hostile artillery is very active at night on the back areas, but no casualties are caused. 2/Lieut. J. McKECHNIE proceeds on leave.	
	26.10.18		Fine autumn day. Companies carry out a little training in the morning, and in the evening start digging positions in the reserve line. Preparations are made for relieving the front line. Hostile artillery again active during the night.	
	27.10.18		Companies carry out training during the morning. Orders to relieve the 6th Somerset L.I. in the front line tomorrow are received.	

D. D. & L., London, E.C.
(A10266) W1 W5300/P713 750,000 2/18 Sch. 52 Forms/C2118/16.

Instructions regarding War Diaries and Intelligence Summaries are contained in F. S. Regs., Part II. and the Staff Manual respectively. Title pages will be prepared in manuscript.

WAR DIARY
~~or~~
INTELLIGENCE SUMMARY.
(Erase heading not required.)

Army Form C. 2118.

Place	Date	Hour	Summary of Events and Information	Remarks and references to Appendices
	28.10.18		Capts. G.C. WETHERALL and J.A. STACE return from leave. Companies start moving up the line at 16.45; relief is complete at 22.00, a very well managed relief. The Battalion is disposed on a 3000 yards front with 2 companies (C and D) in front 'A' in Support and 'B' in Reserve. The men and Officers are living mostly in hastily dug trenches and there is not much comfort for anyone. Lieut & Qmr. R.E. DAWSON reports for duty.	
	29.10.18		Heavy gas shelling with yellow cross gas starts at 01.15 in the region of Bn. HQ. and lasts for 2 hours; luckily there are no casualties. The enemy attempts to raid one of 'C' Company's posts at 22.00 but is driven off. A fairly quiet day follows. Bn. HQ is moved in the evening to a large farm some 300 yds. in advance. Considerable shelling with Gas & H.E. of ST. MAUR and in the neighbourhood of 'D' Company HQ.	
	30.10.18		The enemy raid a Lewis Gun Post of D Company at 04.45 after a short artillery bombardment and get off with 2 of our men, after wounding 2 others slightly; the strength of the enemy was about 20 & he apparently rushed the post from the rear. The day is quiet. The casualties altogether in the last 24 hours, 4 of them being gas cases	
	31.10.18		Quiet day. 2 more gas cases. At about 22.00 the enemy starts shelling Bn. HQ. with 4.2 H.V. guns. 1 direct hit is obtained on the room used as mess and orderly room and everyone is forced to take to the cellar. No casualties.	

[signature]
LT. COL.
CDG. 18th BN. GLOUCESTERSHIRE REGT.

D. D. & L., London, E.C.
(A10266) Wt W5300/P713 750,000 2/18 Sch. 52 Forms/C2118/16.

Instructions regarding War Diaries and Intelligence Summaries are contained in F. S. Regs., Part II. and the Staff Manual respectively. Title pages will be prepared in manuscript.

WAR DIARY
or
~~INTELLIGENCE SUMMARY.~~
(Erase heading not required.)

Nov 18 49/6 Vol 4

Army Form C. 2118.

Place	Date	Hour	Summary of Events and Information	Remarks and references to Appendices
In the Field	November 1st		2/Lieut W.A.KERSLAKE returns from a Course. On the whole a quiet day. The Battalion is relieved during the evening by the 34th London Regt. and on relief passes into Support. Relief is complete just before midnight. There is considerable shelling while the relief is in progress but only 1 or 2 casualties are caused. 2/Lieut. REDGERS is admitted to hospital with influenza. So far there has been very few cases among the men. The Battalion is now disposed as follows: H.Qrs. & C. Company in TAINTIGNIES, B & D Companies at LONGUE SAULT & A. Company in ST. MAUR.	J.S.C.
	2nd		The day is spent in resting. Notification is received that CAPT. KING was admitted to Hospital on the 30th of last month. The usual shelling of TAINTIGNIES and the areas occupied by the Companies takes place at night.	J.S.C.
	3rd		The Colonel goes on leave. 2/Lieut PRUETT returns from a Course. A parade Service is held in the School for C. Company & H.Qrs. B. D & C. Companies are taken for work under the R.E. in the afternoon and evening, Digging the Main Line of Resistance.	J.S.C.
	4th		Lieut SAXTON goes on leave. 2/Lieut FARROW returns from a Course. B, C & D Companies are required for work during the afternoon and evening. The Battalion is relieved rather unexpectedly by the 6/SOM.L.I. in the afternoon & passes into reserve, the same position being occupied as were taken up on our first arrival here. Relief is complete by 21.00.	J.S.C.
	5th		2/Lieut ROSE is admitted to Hospital with influenza. Two Companies are required for work during the afternoon & evening. Preparations are made for relief tomorrow. The total casualties in the Battalion during the 12 days in which the Brigade has held the front line are 1 Killed, 13 wounded and 2 missing.	J.S.C.
	6th		We are relieved by the 18th Scottish Rifles, relief being complete at 11.00. On relief we return to BACHY and occupy roughly the same billets as before. A pouring wet day.	J.S.C.
	7th		The day is devoted to interior economy and providing baths for the men. In the afternoon orders are received that we are to interchange billets with the 34th. London Regt. at SENTIER, about 2 miles EAST of BACHY. At a Conference of Commanding Officers held at Brigade H.Qrs. at 17.15, instructions are given for an attack by this Division in conjunction with others on its flanks to take place on the 11th with the object of crossing the SCHELDT.	J.S.C.

D. D. & L., London, E.C.
(A10266) W1 W5300/P713 750,000 2/18 Sch. 52 Forms/C2118/16.

Instructions regarding War Diaries and Intelligence Summaries are contained in F. S. Regs., Part II. and the Staff Manual respectively. Title pages will be prepared in manuscript.

WAR DIARY
or
~~INTELLIGENCE SUMMARY.~~

(*Erase heading not required.*)

Army Form C. 2118.

Place	Date	Hour	Summary of Events and Information	Remarks and references to Appendices
In the Field	November 8th		During the early morning the Germans retire over the SCHELDT and the order for us to change billets is cancelled. We are put under 1 hours notice to move. 2/Lieuts. HODGES & DURANT are admitted to Hospital with influenza. A pouring wet day.	[illegible]
	9th		Training is started in earnest. Classes for Lewis Gunners, Signallers, Scouts and a class of young N.C.O's under the Regimental Sergeant-Major are assembled. Companies carry out training independently, special attention being paid to Advanced Guard and Outpost Schemes.	[illegible]
	10th		Orders received at 03.00 that we are to move forward to day. The Battalion leaves for WEZ-VELVAIN at 10.30, marching by RUMES - FLORENT - TAINTIGNIES and GUIGNIES: we arrive at 15.00, having had dinner on the way. The Village is considerably knocked about by shell fire and all the houses have been disgracefully looted. Major B.K. COOKE. M.C is admitted to hospital with influenza and CAPT. G.C. WETHERALL takes over Command.	[illegible]
	11th		At 9 A.M. – no – 0900 hours the expected wire arrives ordering the cessation of hostilities as from 11.00 hours. The news spreads like wildfire round the Battn. but no one seems to realise its full significance and training for war proceeds apace. Maj. Gen Ritchie. G.O.C. 16th Division calls to wish the Battalion "the very best of luck on this memorable day". Respirators, small box, are cast aside with many sighs of relief, and the remainder of the day is given over to football etc. Beyond the usual diminutive issue of rum no stimulating beverages of any description are available, and the nocturnal celebrations are therefore comparatively quiet throughout the Battalion.	[illegible]
	12th		Battalion "standing to" awaiting orders, meanwhile training proceeds. Orderly Room besieged all day by returning civilians desirous of requisitioning the Battalion transport for the purpose of transporting hither their goods from all parts of France and Belgium. Having fallen a victim to the ever present 'flue' the Adjutant	[illegible]

D. D. & L., London, E.C.
(A10266) Wt W5300/P713 750,000 2/18 Sch. 52 Forms/C2118/16.

Instructions regarding War Diaries and Intelligence Summaries are contained in F. S. Regs., Part II. and the Staff Manual respectively. Title pages will be prepared in manuscript.

WAR DIARY
or
INTELLIGENCE SUMMARY
(Erase heading not required.)

Army Form C. 2118.

Place	Date	Hour	Summary of Events and Information	Remarks and references to Appendices
In the Field	Nov. 12 contd.		disappears westwards in an ambulance car and the Assistant Adjutant takes over the reins of Office. In the evening the Battn. Concert Party, "under the able direction of 2/Lt Fuller" & under the distinguished patronage of Brig. Gen. E. P. Nash. DSO., the Actg. Staff Captain (Lieut. H.N. Parker) and many other celebrities, surpasses all its previous achievements, the scene of operations being the CONVENT at WEZ-VELVAIN, a splendid hall with no lack of ventilation and an extraordinary lighting installation of some 55 candle power arranged by the Q.M. Staff.	[illegible]
	13th		The whole Battalion parades at 10.00 in the Convent for a Thanksgiving Service conducted by the C. of E & Nonconformist padres jointly. Remainder of the day is devoted to recreational training and games.	[illegible]
	14th		News of a forthcoming Brigade Ceremonial Parade and march past having filtered through, the Battalion parades for Ceremonial Drill. Arms drill excellent but march past might be better. In the afternoon the Battn Soccer team takes on the South African heavy gunners and a fast exciting game ends in a draw of 2 goals all.	[illegible]
	15th		The Battalion receives orders to move to MOUCHIN and proceeds there by a long and somewhat tortuous route partly owing to the obstructions placed in our way by the Boche, and partly owing to the fact that the Signalling Officer led the way. However despite all the latter's attempts to lead us astray (some of which were unfortunately too successful) the Battn. arrives in time for Lunch. Billets are quite good and the inhabitants are very kindly disposed to the men.	[illegible]
	16th		Battalion moves to MONS-EN-PEVELE a march of approximately 16 kilometres. Every man is in by 15.30 and B.G.C. expresses his satisfaction with manner in which march was carried out. Good billets.	[illegible]
	17th		Very quiet day. Owing to intense cold and absence of a suitable room, no Parade Service is held, but the Padre holds a Voluntary Service in the School, and also a "Smoker" Service in the evening.	[illegible]
	18th		Another quiet - and cold - day. Companies do 2 hours training in the morning and also hear a lecture on the popular subject of "Demobilisation and Reconstruction" by the Battn. Education Officer (Lt. Jackson). The afternoon is spent in football & inter-Company Cross Country runs.	[illegible]

(A10266) Wt W5300/P713 750,000 2/18 Sch. 52 Forms/C2118/16. D. D. & L., London, E.C.

Instructions regarding War Diaries and Intelligence Summaries are contained in F. S. Regs., Part II. and the Staff Manual respectively. Title pages will be prepared in manuscript.

WAR DIARY
or
INTELLIGENCE SUMMARY.
(Erase heading not required.)

Army Form C. 2118.

Place	Date	Hour	Summary of Events and Information	Remarks and references to Appendices
	NOV.			
In the Field	19th		A quiet and still colder day, mainly spent in trying to get warm by means of the system introduced by one "O'Grady" of P.T. fame. Major Cooke returns from Hospital. Capt. Holt from 1st Corps School, & Lt. R.T. Wilson joins the Battn during the day. Major Cooke takes over Command and Capt Weatherall assumes the duties of 2nd in Command.	YGC
	20th		Training of a mild character continues, and "education" is in full swing. As far as the latter subject is concerned, the Battn has made great strides, the Educational Officer reporting that a man does not exist in the unit who can not spell CAT. The C.O. Capt. Jacks & Lt. Jackson attend a conference at Bde. H.Qrs on Educational and sporting matters. 2/Lieut. A.E. Sansom joins the Battalion.	YGC
	21st		Training continues, consisting of P.T. close order drill & Educational Classes. All Lewis Guns are inspected and overhauled during the day.	YGC
	22nd		Training continues & includes Specialist Classes. A Guard mounting Demonstration is held on the Square attended by all Subalterns and N.C.O's. The promotion of Capt L.C. Wetherall to T/Major is announced and is duly celebrated.	YGC
	23rd		Training continues as usual, the afternoon being given over to games. Very cold day. The fumigator arrives & deals successfully with A. Coy & H.Q. blankets.	YGC
	24th		The fumigator continues its activities and the blankets of B.C. & D. Coys lose their mobility. Parties from A & D Coys attend Parade Service at the School wearing great-coats, & even then looking very cold. 2/Lieut. Pruett proceeds to 1st Army Musketry Camp on a course and Capt Jacks goes on leave.	YGC
	25th		Training continues, Companies afterwards dispersing in search of Salvage. Our Area seems to be entirely devoid of interesting material requiring to be Salved. Our first days haul consists of 1 iron screw picket & 1660 x Twine.	YGC
	26th		Training and salvage continues and much useful material is brought in to-day. Specialist Classes in full swing.	YGC
	27th		Training and Specialist & Educational Classes continue. Col Barwell rejoins from leave and resumes command of the Battn. Major Cooke resumes duties of 2nd in Command, whilst Major Wetherall becomes O.C. Xmas Dinners.	YGC

(A10266) Wt W5300/P713 750,000 2/18 Sch. 52 Forms/C2118/16. D. D. & L., London, E.C.

Instructions regarding War Diaries and Intelligence Summaries are contained in F. S. Regs., Part II. and the Staff Manual respectively. Title pages will be prepared in manuscript.

WAR DIARY
or
~~INTELLIGENCE SUMMARY.~~

(Erase heading not required.)

Army Form C. 2118.

Place	Date	Hour	Summary of Events and Information	Remarks and references to Appendices
In the Field	Nov 28th		Training and Salvage continues, the latter under the supervision of Lt. Saxton. C.O. inspects D. Coy. on parade. Clothes require alteration in the case of the majority of the men.	[initials]
	29th		C & D Coys. continue training. A & B Coys after inspection by the C.O. march to DEUX VILLES to prepare the Brewery for their entry on the morrow. A party of woodcutters under Sgt. Hughes commence their attack on the BOIS del' OFFLANDE in order to provide a sufficiency of fuel for the winter. N.C.O's recommend for promotion are paraded for C.O's inspection, and the few vacancies are filled.	[initials]
	30th		C.O. inspects C. Coy. on parade - clothing again requiring much alteration. A and B. Coys move to the Brewery at DEUX VILLES and settle in very comfortably. Companies at disposal of Coy. Commanders for training. Afternoon given over to football.	[initials]

[signature] Lieut-Col. [illegible]
18th Gloucester Regt.

D. D. & L., London, E.C.
(A10266) Wt W5300/P713 750,000 2/18 Sch. 52 Forms/C2118/16.

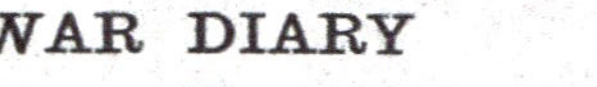

Instructions regarding War Diaries and Intelligence Summaries are contained in F. S. Regs., Part II. and the Staff Manual respectively. Title pages will be prepared in manuscript.

WAR DIARY
or
~~INTELLIGENCE SUMMARY.~~
(Erase heading not required.)

Army Form C. 2118.

VR 5

Place	Date	Hour	Summary of Events and Information	Remarks and references to Appendices
	1-12-18		Church Parade is held in the Brewery, DEUX VILLES. The Brigadier attended & the Staff Captain, is present and reads the lesson. All the men are in good voice and the service is quite a success even the sermon is not quite so dull as usual. The Brigadier takes the opportunity of walking round DEUX VILLES and seems comparatively satisfied with what he sees.	
	2-12-18		Training continues and "Education" is in full swing, whilst King Football holds sway in the afternoon.	
	3-12-18		The Battn. assembles during the morning near BELLECAMPS CHATEAU and proceeds to execute various manoeuvres. Drill quite good. In the afternoon H.Q. Coy parades "en masse" in the square and it is at last settled who is a H.Q. and who isn't.	
	4-12-18		Training continues, and includes guard mounting practice and indoor schemes on sand table. Orders to help the Local Farmers as much as possible in the farming of their land having been received, the 4 cooker teams are turned out and each do 4 hours ploughing on farms in the vicinity. A very interesting lecture is given by Brig. Gen. Nash. DSO. on "Soldiering in India under Peace conditions" in the evening. C. Coy Dining Room is well filled for the occasion and the lecture much appreciated. Very good Guard provided by D. Coy to-day.	
	5-12-18		The Battn. in company with the remainder of the Brigade is reviewed by Brig. Gen. Nash. DSO Commdg. on the Aerodrome, BERSEE. In spite of a fairly strong breeze which makes it very difficult to hear the words of command, the inspection and subsequent march past are quite well carried out, and Gen. Nash expresses his satisfaction with same. The Divnl Band plays in the Square during the afternoon & also for Ceremonial Guard mounting for which C. Coy. provide a smartly turned out guard.	J.R.
	6-12-18		Owing to the rain it is found necessary to cancel the Company Competitions arranged for this morning, and the troops instead attend lectures in their various dining rooms. Lieut A.H. BEATTIE is admitted to Hospl. and 2/Lt. R.C. WHITE assumes the duties of Transport Officer. Lieut K.C. LEMON and 2/Lieut G.M. HIGGS join the Battn from the 2/1st Gloucester Hussars.	J.R.
	7-12-18		No parades to-day so most of the time is spent in football etc. Sgt KIPPAX takes over the duties of Provost Sergt.	J.R.
	8-12-18		Parade Services are held in the Brewery DEUX VILLES for C of E. men and in the School MONS-EN-PEVELE for non-conformists. Lieut A. GORRINGE receives permission to wear the badges of Captn. under Sec. II C.A.S. 384.	J.R.
	10-12-18		The Battn parades at 9 and then goes a short route march as far as MERIGNIES and back — men march very well and sing the whole way round.	J.R.
	9-12-18		Company training continues.	J.R.

D. D. & L., London, E.C.
(A10266) Wt W5300/P713 750,000 2/18 Sch. 52 Forms/C2118/16.

Instructions regarding War Diaries and Intelligence Summaries are contained in F. S. Regs., Part II. and the Staff Manual respectively. Title pages will be prepared in manuscript.

WAR DIARY
or
INTELLIGENCE SUMMARY.
(Erase heading not required.)

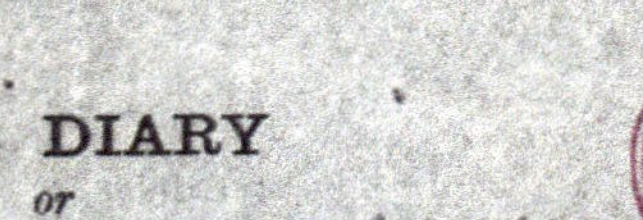

Army Form C. 2118.

Place	Date	Hour	Summary of Events and Information	Remarks and references to Appendices
	11-12-18		Fifteen Officers and about a hundred other ranks attend at the Lecture Hall at 10. a.m. in anticipation of a lecture on "Anglo-American Relations" but after an hours wait, they return home cold and not a little annoyed, the lecturer having failed to put in an appearance. In the meantime the 2nd in Command, Adjutant and a few kindred spirits attend the I Corps Race Meeting at MOUCHIN being conveyed thither by a Motor Lorry which after a somewhat eventful journey deposits them safe, but not a little shaken, on the Course. Here a very enjoyable day is spent the meeting being very well arranged. Col Barwell leaves the Battn to proceed to Camberley on a 6 weeks course & Major B.K. Cooke M.C. assumes Command. Major Wethereall taking over the latters duties as 2 R.I. etc. Lieut Beattie T.O. returns from Hospital.	J.R.
	12-12-18		Company training continues, including Guard mounting practice. D Coy send a platoon to work on the old German range & make it fit for use. Lieut G.C. CHATE joins the Battn.	J.R.
	13-12-18		Training continues as usual. A Lorry having been placed at our disposal, a party of 2 Officers & 26 men are sent in to LILLE for the day, & return apparently having had a good, if somewhat short, time there.	J.R.
	14-12-18		Training and Salvage work continues. A very depressing day indeed.	J.R.
	15-12-18		The usual parade Services are held, and in the afternoon, the Battn is unfortunately knocked out of the Divl. Football Competition by the 16th M.G. Battn by 4 goals to nil our eleven being quite off their game.	J.R.
	16-12-18		Training and Salvage work continues.	J.R.
	17-12-18		The Battn parades near the Windmill on the BERSEE Road and carries out Ceremonial Drill. Men are quite keen and the drill is well done.	J.R.
	18-12-18		Training and Salvage work as usual.	J.R.
	19-12-18		Training continues and another Lorry-load of Officers and men are sent to LILLE for the day all of whom return laden with Xmas goods etc.	J.R.
	20-12-18		Battn takes part in a Brigade Route march, the route being LE PAVÉ, NEUVEAU JEU, MERIGNIES and home. Rather cold day but men are cheerful & march well.	J.R.
	21-12-18		Company training & salvage work continues. The Battn Library & Reading Room is opened at MONS-EN-PEVELE and bids fair to become a very popular institution. Lieut A.G. LEGG joins the Battn.	J.R.
	22-12-18		Parade Services are held as usual and in the afternoon the Battn football eleven succeeds in turning tables on the M.G. Battn to the tune of 5 goals to 2.	J.R.
	23-12-18		Training continues, the Right half Battn practising "Deployment" at DEUX VILLES, the 2 other Coys doing Lewis Gun training. An "Army Class" under Major Wethereall is started for men continuing in the Army.	J.R.

(A10266) Wt W5300/P713 750,000 2/18 Sch. 52 Forms/C2118/16. D. D. & L., London, E.C.

Army Form C. 2118.

Instructions regarding War Diaries and Intelligence Summaries are contained in F. S. Regs., Part II. and the Staff Manual respectively. Title pages will be prepared in manuscript.

WAR DIARY
or
~~INTELLIGENCE SUMMARY.~~
(Erase heading not required.)

Place	Date	Hour	Summary of Events and Information	Remarks and references to Appendices
	24-12-18		The Battn parades at DEUXVILLES and then proceeds on a route march through THUMERIES returning home via LA PETRIE. The afternoon is spent in putting up Xmas Decorations etc.	
	25-12-18		Xmas Day. Church parade is held in the Concert Hall, MONS-EN-PEVELE, and is followed by a celebration of Holy Communion. During the course of the day the Commanding Officer visits each Company at dinner. Everyone is in excellent spirits, and the Q.M., [illegible] and his assistants have surpassed themselves as far as the dinner is concerned. At the Church Service a collection was made on behalf of the Red Cross Society.	J.R.
	26-12-18		Training was carried out for 1 hour only owing to the Div: Steeplechase meeting being held on this day. Several Officers rode to the ground in a four-in-hand G.S. Wagon driven by Major B.K. Cooke, M.C. The party included a bugler whose efforts on the instrument were somewhat very much below expectation. The meeting was a very successful one, especially for one of the Junior Subalterns, whose spirits on the homeward journey were very high.	J.R.
	27-12-18		Training and Salvage work as usual. A house to house search was made to salvage all arms and ammunition left behind by the Boche. The search was fairly successful.	
	28-12-18		Company training and Salvage work as usual.	J.R.
	29-12-18		Parade Services as usual. No football was played owing to the grounds being under water through recent heavy rain.	J.R.
	30-12-18		Training and Salvage as usual.	J.R.
	31-12-18		Training &c as usual. A Lecture on "The Individual and the Nation's Health" in the Theatre was given, which was attended by 1 Officer and 24 O.R. per Company. Capt. L.H. Keng, M.C. rejoined for duty.	J.R.

B. Kennedy Cooke Major
Comdg. 18th BN. GLOUCESTERSHIRE REGT.

49th Inf. Bde. H.Q.

Herewith War Diary for the Unit under my Command for the month of January. 1919

[signature]

Lt. Col.

Commanding 18th Gloster Regt.

4/2/19

Instructions regarding War Diaries and Intelligence Summaries are contained in F. S. Regs., Part II. and the Staff Manual respectively. Title pages will be prepared in manuscript.

WAR DIARY
~~or~~
~~INTELLIGENCE SUMMARY.~~
(Erase heading not required.)

Army Form C. 2118.

FTP 16

18 Gloucester

Vol 6

Place	Date 1919	Hour	Summary of Events and Information	Remarks and references to Appendices
	1st Jan		By the wish of the B.G.C. 48th Inf Bde this day is given over to sports etc. and no parades are held.	
	2nd		Training and Salvage work continues under Coy arrangements. The Battn. Football XI went down to the representatives of the 36th London Regt. in the afternoon and a good game [illegible]	
	3rd		The Battn. takes part in a Brigade Route March via LE PARADIS and RUE COUETTE. The drums appear once more and play quite well. Men very cheerful and march well. Lt (A/Capt) W.H. SIMMONDS joins the Battn.	
	4th		Training and Salvage work as usual. Capt. L.T. Addington temporarily assumes the duties of Area Commandant. Capt W.H. King, M.C. takes over "D" Coy.	J.B.
	5th		Parade Services are held as usual.	
	6th		Training and Salvage work continue. The Brigadier and his staff dine with the Regt.	
	7th		The Battn. marches to PONT-A-MARCQ and back in good time. A conference of Officers is held for the purpose of discussing the equipment of infantry in future wars, the views of the conference being sent forward. The [illegible] receives permission from G.O.C. [illegible] to wear badges of rank of Captain. A successful concert is given in the Concert Hall, MONS-EN-PÉVÈLE the G.O.C. being present.	
	8th		Training and Salvage work continues as usual.	

I.O.
Gotata

D. D. & L., London, E.C.
(A10266) Wt W5300/P713 750,000 2/18 Sch. 52 Forms/C2118/16.

Instructions regarding War Diaries and Intelligence Summaries are contained in F. S. Regs., Part II. and the Staff Manual respectively. Title pages will be prepared in manuscript.

WAR DIARY

~~or~~

~~INTELLIGENCE~~ SUMMARY.

(*Erase heading not required.*)

Army Form C. 2118.

Place	Date 1919	Hour	Summary of Events and Information	Remarks and references to Appendices
	9th Jan		Training and salvage work as usual. The Battn. Football XI visited the 6th Somerset Light Infantry in the afternoon and a well contested game ended in a victory of 2 goals to nil in favour of the Somersets. Capt. [illegible] Holt, M.C. proceeds to U.K. on the Senior Officers Course, and Capt. King M.C. takes over command of "D" Coy. 2/Lt. J. McKechnie assumes command of "A" Coy.	[illegible]
	10th		Brigade training being cancelled the morning was devoted to salvage work. Much material was obtained from the new area.	
	11th		Company training and salvage work continued as usual.	
	12th		Parade Services as usual.	
	13th		Training and salvage work continued as usual.	
	14th		To-day was devoted to salvage work. A large quantity of material was salved. 2/Lt. R. C. White assumed the duties of Transport Officer vice Lieut. A. W. Beattie to U.K. on leave 11.1.19.	
	15th		Training and salvage work continued as usual.	
	16th		To-day was selected for the inspection of [illegible]. The turn-out of the Battalion [illegible] was excellent and the Commanding Officer commended them on their smartness.	
	17th		The Brigade Day being cancelled the Battn. carried out a Route March via LA [illegible] PETIT ATTICHES, LA NEUVILLE, THUMERIES and home. The march was about 9 miles and the men were cheerful and marched well.	

D. D. & L., London, E.C.
(A10266) Wt W5300/P713 750,000 2/18 Sch. 52 Forms/C2118/16.

Instructions regarding War Diaries and Intelligence Summaries are contained in F. S. Regs., Part II. and the Staff Manual respectively. Title pages will be prepared in manuscript.

WAR DIARY
or
INTELLIGENCE SUMMARY.
(Erase heading not required.)

Army Form C. 2118.

Place	Date 1919	Hour	Summary of Events and Information	Remarks and references to Appendices
	18th Jany		Training and salvage continues as usual. 2/Lt L.O. Toms returned from Leave	
	19th		Parade services as usual	
	20th		Training & salvage work continues as usual	
	21st		The Battn. Day was cancelled and Coys were at the disposal of the respective Commanders 2/Lt. J. Peagus assumes the duties of A/Adjutant vice Capt. [illegible] [illegible] Capt. J.H. [illegible] assumes the duties of Educational Officer vice Lieut. J.H. Jackson demobilized [illegible]	
	22nd		Training and salvage work continues. Lieut. Col. [illegible] Barwell M.C. having returned from a course M.C. resumes Command of the Battn.	[illegible]
	23rd		Training & salvage work continues as usual.	
	24th		The Battalion takes part in a Brigade route march via [illegible] BERSEE – FAUMONT – MONCHEAUX – and back to billets. The Battalion Concert Party (Old [illegible]) gave a Concert in the evening which was attended by a large number of the Battalion. This was the first show given by the Party and it was a great success. Capt. Corrigan returned from Leave.	
	25th		Training and salvage work is continued	

D. D. & L., London, E.C.
(A10266) Wt W5300/P713 750,000 2/18 Sch. 52 Forms/C2118/16.

Instructions regarding War Diaries and Intelligence Summaries are contained in F. S. Regs., Part II. and the Staff Manual respectively. Title pages will be prepared in manuscript.

WAR DIARY

~~or~~

~~INTELLIGENCE~~ SUMMARY.

(Erase heading not required.)

Army Form C. 2118.

Place	Date 1919	Hour	Summary of Events and Information	Remarks and references to Appendices
	26th Jan		Parade services as usual.	
	27th		Training & Salvage Work continued	
	28th		Snow fell heavily during the night and Salvage Work was cancelled.	
	29th		The morning was devoted to Photography. The Official Photographer from [illegible] photographed the Battalion in various groups.	
	30th		A memorial service was celebrated in the Church, MONS-EN-PEVELE in memory of ADOLPHE PLAISANT Cpl. in the 1st Regiment of Infantry killed in action Dec 31st 1914. At this memorial service the Battalion was invited to take part. The Battalion was represented by the Commanding Officer, Adjutant, Regt. Sgt. Major and 20 other ranks.	[illegible]
			The Battalion was paraded in the Square MONS-EN-PEVELE at 09.30 hours for the purpose of an address by the Commanding Officer. Lieut. A.G. Legg assumed the duties of Education Officer vice Capt. [illegible] on leave U.K. Lieut. A.H. [illegible] rejoined the Battn. from [illegible] and resumed the duty of [illegible] Officer. [illegible] Heath rejoined the Battalion from leave to U.K. and assumed Command of "B" Coy and [illegible] Detachment.	

D. D. & L., London, E.C.
(A10266) Wt W5300/P713 750,000 2/18 Sch. 52 Forms/C2118/16.

Instructions regarding War Diaries and Intelligence Summaries are contained in F. S. Regs., Part II. and the Staff Manual respectively. Title pages will be prepared in manuscript.

WAR DIARY

~~or~~

~~INTELLIGENCE SUMMARY.~~

(Erase heading not required.)

Army Form C. 2118.

Place	Date 1919	Hour	Summary of Events and Information	Remarks and references to Appendices
	31st Jan		Training was carried out for 1 hour after which men were engaged in clearing snow from roads and gutters under company arrangements. A concert party from the [illegible] Somerset Light Infantry performed in the theatre, [illegible] in the evening and there was a good attendance.	

[illegible] A/Lt Col

Commanding 18th Batt. [illegible] Regt.

D. D. & L., London, E.C. (A10266) Wt W5300/P713 750,000 2/18 Sch. 52 Forms/C2118/16.

2.0

18 Gloucester
SW 7

Instructions regarding War Diaries and Intelligence Summaries are contained in F. S. Regs., Part II. and the Staff Manual respectively. Title pages will be prepared in manuscript.

WAR DIARY
or
~~INTELLIGENCE SUMMARY.~~

(Erase heading not required.)

Army Form C. 2118.

Place	Date 1919	Hour	Summary of Events and Information	Remarks and references to Appendices
	1st Feby		The Battn paraded for practice of Ceremonial Drill in preparation for the presentation of the King's Colour.	LR
	2nd "		Parade Services as usual.	LR
	3rd "		The Battalion owing to its numbers diminishing through demobilization is organised into 2 Companies No 1 & No. 2 Coys.	LR
	4th "		The Battn paraded and marched to BERSEE to take part in the Brigade rehearsal for the consecration and presentation of the King's Colour. The Commanding Officer gave a lecture to the Battalion at DEUX VILLES. Subject "Demobilization and after". This was appreicated by all ranks. Lieut K. C. Lemon, assumes the duties of Asst/Adjt with effect from 21.1.19.	LR
	5th "		A Memorial Service was celebrated at the Church MONS EN PEVELE in memory of GEORGE POCQUET Private in the French Army.	LR

D. D. & L., London, E.C.
(A10266) Wt W5300/P713 750,000 2/18 Sch. 52 Forms/C2118/16.

Instructions regarding War Diaries and Intelligence Summaries are contained in F. S. Regs., Part II. and the Staff Manual respectively. Title pages will be prepared in manuscript.

WAR DIARY or ~~INTELLIGENCE SUMMARY.~~

(Erase heading not required.)

Army Form C. 2118.

Place	Date 1919	Hour	Summary of Events and Information	Remarks and references to Appendices
	5th Feby.		Killed in Action. Dec 12th 1916.	
			At this Memorial Service the Battalion was represented by Capt W. H. King M.C., Lieut Saxton, and 1 Sergt, 1 Cpl & 3 private Soldiers.	LR
	6th Feby.		The Consecration & presentation of the King's Colour was cancelled owing to the weather being so cold & severe.	LR
	7th "		The Consecration and presentation of the King's Colour took place today. The presentation was given by Lieut General Sir Arthur Holland K.C.B. D.S.O. M.V.O. Commanding I Corps.	LR
	8th "		The Commanding Officer desires to put on record his appreciation of the turn out and smartness shewn by all ranks on the Colour parade, yesterday.	LR
			Training was carried out under Coy. arrangements.	
	9th "		Parade Services as usual.	LR
	10th "		The Battalion is arranging for an inter-Battn. move.	LR

D. D. & L., London, E.C.
(A10266) Wt W5300/P713 750,000 2/18 Sch. 52 Forms/C2118/16.

Instructions regarding War Diaries and Intelligence Summaries are contained in F. S. Regs., Part II. and the Staff Manual respectively. Title pages will be prepared in manuscript.

WAR DIARY
or
~~INTELLIGENCE SUMMARY.~~

(Erase heading not required.)

Army Form C. 2118.

Place	Date 1919.	Hour	Summary of Events and Information	Remarks and references to Appendices
	11th Feb		Training is carried out under Coy. arrangements.	LR
	12th "		Training is carried out under Coy. arrangements.	LR
	13th "		Training is carried out under Coy. arrangements.	LR
	14th "		There were no parades today.	
			A ceremonial guard mounting took place on the Square. MONS EN PEVELE. at Retreat. The Kings Colour was present. The parade was commanded by Major G. C. Wetherall.	LR
	15th "		The were no parades today. Capt J. A. Stace takes over the duty of Education Officer vice Lieut Legg to U. K. Draft Conducting. The Commanding Officer gave a lecture to all ranks at DEUX VILLES	LR
	16th "		Parade Services as usual.	LR
	17th "		The inter-Battalion move took place today. The detachment at DEUX VILLES now comprises of the draft and other attached personnel, under Capt O. L. Jacks M.C.	LR
	18th "		The Education Officer arranged Educational Classes for all ranks, except those engaged on administrative or other special duties.	LR

D. D. & L., London, E.C.
(A10266) Wt W5300/P713 750,000 2/18 Sch. 52 Forms/C2118/16.

Instructions regarding War Diaries and Intelligence Summaries are contained in F. S. Regs., Part II. and the Staff Manual respectively. Title pages will be prepared in manuscript.

WAR DIARY
or
INTELLIGENCE SUMMARY.
(Erase heading not required.)

Army Form C. 2118.

Place	Date 1919	Hour	Summary of Events and Information	Remarks and references to Appendices
	19th Feb.		Training under Coy. Arrangements.	LR
	20		Interior economy was carried out. A fatigue party for daily woodcutting commenced today.	LR
	21st		All available ranks were employed on clearing roads of mud caused by the thaw.	LR
	22nd		The Commanding Officer inspected the Draft Coy. after which they proceeded on a short route march.	
			The personnel of the 49th Light Trench Mortar Battery are attached to the Batt: for:- pay, rations, clothing, discipline, & training with effect from 18.2.19 same to be administered as an attached Company under command of Capt. J.A. Curtois.	LR
			2nd Lieutenants White & Brameld carried out a tour of survey of, & made a report on, such billets as have at any time been occupied by the Battalion.	
	23rd		Parade services as usual.	LR
			The Battalion Transport was inspected by the Commanding Officer.	

D. D. & L., London, E.C.
(A10266) Wt W5300/P713 750,000 2/18 Sch. 52 Forms/C2118/16.

Instructions regarding War Diaries and Intelligence Summaries are contained in F. S. Regs., Part II. and the Staff Manual respectively. Title pages will be prepared in manuscript.

WAR DIARY
or
~~INTELLIGENCE SUMMARY.~~
(Erase heading not required.)

Army Form C. 2118.

Place	Date 1919.	Hour	Summary of Events and Information	Remarks and references to Appendices
	24th Feb.		There were no parades today.	
	25th.		2nd Lt. R. Hill, 2nd Lt. L. S. Toms, & 120 other ranks all of whom are volunteers for the Army of Occupation, marched to Lille to entrain for Rouen to join the 2/5 Batt: Gloucestershire Regiment.	LR
			All Billets at DEUX VILLES were evacuated.	LR
			The Battalion will be administered as one Company under Command of Capt. F. D. Heath, with effect from 26.2.19.	
	26th.		Owing to the Battalion being further diminished, all ranks are employed on administrative or other special duties.	
			Lieut K. C. Lemon rejoined from Leave.	LR
			A Concert was given in the Concert Hall, by The Lena Ashwell Concert Party, The Concert Hall was packed, The Concert was very good, & the audience showed great appreciation of same.	
	27th.		2nd Lieut A. E. Sansom rejoined from Leave.	
	28th.		The Divisional Steeplechase meeting was held at Bersee, at which several of our Officers were present, some of whom were driven there in a four-in-hand G.S. Wagon.	LR

D. D. & L., London, E.C.
(A10266) Wt W5300/P713 750,000 2/18 Sch. 52 Forms/C2118/16.

Instructions regarding War Diaries and Intelligence Summaries are contained in F. S. Regs., Part II. and the Staff Manual respectively. Title pages will be prepared in manuscript.

WAR DIARY
or
~~INTELLIGENCE~~ SUMMARY.
(Erase heading not required.)

Army Form C. 2118.

Place	Date	Hour	Summary of Events and Information	Remarks and references to Appendices
	1919.			LR
	26th Feb.		Major B. K. Cooke M.C. + Lieut A. M. Beatie taking the ribbons in turn, both of whom displayed great skill at their task, particularly on the homeward journey.	

[signature]
Lieut. Colonel
Commanding 18th Gloucester Regiment.

D. D. & L., London, E.C.
(A10266) Wt W5300/P713 750,000 2/18 Sch. 52 Forms/C2118/16.

Instructions regarding War Diaries and Intelligence Summaries are contained in F. S. Regs., Part II, and the Staff Manual respectively. Title pages will be prepared in manuscript.

WAR DIARY
or
~~INTELLIGENCE SUMMARY.~~
(Erase heading not required.)

Army Form C. 2118.

18 Gloucester

9/8. 8

Place	Date	Hour	Summary of Events and Information	Remarks and references to Appendices
	1919 March			
Mons-en-Pevele	1st		There are no events of note to record today	JR
	2nd		The Services today were voluntary.	JR
	3rd		There are no events of note to record today.	JR
			7 Horses & 2 Mules were despatched to Tournai	JR.
	4th		There are no events of note to record today.	JR
	5th		There are no events of note to record today.	JR
			11. Horses were despatched to Bersee	
	6th		There are no events of note to record today	JR
	7th		2nd Lieut J. S. Durant rejoins from Base	JR
	8th		The Division held a Steeplechase Meeting at Bersee. All other ranks were paraded & marched to same.	JR
			3 L. D. Horses class B. 2 were sold by Auction in a Sale held at Mons-en-Pevele.	
	9th		The Services today were voluntary.	JR
	10th		2nd Lieut J McKechnie rejoined from Leave	JR

3c 0
[illegible]

D. D. & L., London, E.C.
(A7883) Wt W809/M1672 350,000 4/17 Sch. 52a Forms/C/2118/14

Instructions regarding War Diaries and Intelligence Summaries are contained in F. S. Regs., Part II, and the Staff Manual respectively. Title pages will be prepared in manuscript.

WAR DIARY
or
~~INTELLIGENCE SUMMARY.~~
(Erase heading not required.)

Army Form C. 2118.

Place	Date	Hour	Summary of Events and Information	Remarks and references to Appendices
	March 1919			
Mons-en-Pevele	11th		2nd Lieut J S Durant proceeded to join No. 196. Prisoner of War Coy, Abbeville Area.	LR
	12th		All other ranks of the 49th L.T.M.B. proceeded to rejoin their Units, except one other Rank forming the Cadre.	LR
			2nd Lieut Koenig, Royal Engineers, is attached to the Batt: for rations & accommodation whilst performing duties of valuation.	
	13th		Capt W. H. King is appointed to take charge of the men's messing.	LR
			Lieut H. C. Lemon, assumes the duties of A/Adjt. vice Capt J Rodgers, leave to U.K. 13-3-19.	
	14th		There is no events of note to record today.	LR
	15th		There is no events of note to record today.	LR
	16th		Capt O. L. Jacks M.C. & Lt A. M. Beattie proceed on demobilization	LR
			2nd Lt R. C. White takes over duties of Transport Officer vice Lt A. M. Beattie	
			The Services today were voluntary.	
	17th		There are no events of note to record today	LR
	18th		The Battalion commence to move all Stores etc to TEMPLEUVE, prior to the move of the CADRE.	LR

D. D. & L., London, E.C. (A7883) Wt W809/M1672 350,000 4/17 Sch 52a Forms/C/2118/14

WAR DIARY
or
~~INTELLIGENCE SUMMARY.~~
(Erase heading not required.)

Army Form C. 2118.

Instructions regarding War Diaries and Intelligence Summaries are contained in F. S. Regs., Part II. and the Staff Manual respectively. Title pages will be prepared in manuscript.

Place	Date	Hour	Summary of Events and Information	Remarks and references to Appendices
	1919			
[illegible]	19 Mch		There are no events of note to record today.	LR
"	20		There are no events of note to record today.	LR
	21		There are no events of note to record today.	LR
	22		Lieut K.C. Lemon and 2/Lt G. [illegible]-Cooke + 83 O.R. left the battalion to proceed to Rouen to join the [illegible] Batt. Gloucestershire Regt.	LR
			Lieut [illegible] rejoined from leave	
			Capt [illegible] assumes the duties of Act. Adjt. vice Lt K.C. Lemon [illegible]	
"	23		There are no events of note to record today.	LR
	24		There are no events of note to record today.	LR
"	25		The Cadre of the Batt. [illegible] attached details [illegible] today.	
			From today the 16th Divisional H.Q. [illegible] under the command of Brigadier-General R.N. BRAY D.S.O. thereby eliminating Divisional and Brigade H.Q.	LR
			Lieut J. McKECHNIE + 2/Lt BRAMFELD proceeded on demobilization.	
			Capt P.A. CURTOIS left to join the 4th Batt SUFFOLKS.	
"	26		There are no events of note to record today.	LR

D. D. & L., London, E.C.
(A7883) Wt. W809/M1672 350,000 4/17 Sch. 52a Forms/C/2118/14

Instructions regarding War Diaries and Intelligence Summaries are contained in F. S. Regs., Part II. and the Staff Manual respectively. Title pages will be prepared in manuscript.

WAR DIARY
or
~~INTELLIGENCE SUMMARY.~~

(Erase heading not required.)

Army Form C. 2118.

Place	Date	Hour	Summary of Events and Information	Remarks and references to Appendices
	1919			
BERSEE	March 27th		There are no events of note to record today.	
	28.		There are no events of note to record today.	
	29.		There are no events of note to record today.	
	30		Capt A. GORRINGE left the Battalion for demobilization	
			Capt J. REDGERS rejoined from Leave.	
	31.		There are no events of note to record today.	

[signature]
Lieut: Colonel
Commanding 18th Bn Gloucester Regt.

D. D. & L., London, E.C.
(A7883) Wt W809/M1672 350,000 4/17 Sch. 52a Forms/C/2118/14

Instructions regarding War Diaries and Intelligence Summaries are contained in F. S. Regs., Part II, and the Staff Manual respectively. Title pages will be prepared in manuscript.

WAR DIARY
or
~~INTELLIGENCE SUMMARY.~~
(Erase heading not required.)

Army Form C. 2118.

18 Gloucester

18 9

Place	Date 1919	Hour	Summary of Events and Information	Remarks and references to Appendices
BERSEE	Apl. 1st		There are no events of note to record today.	
	" 2nd		There are no events of note to record today.	
	" 3rd		A football match was played today between the Battalion and the 7th Dragoons (French Team). After a very exciting and clean game the result was in favour of the Battalion by 3 goals to 2.	
	" 4th		There are no events of note to record today.	
	" 5th		A lorry was allotted to the Brigade Cadres for the purpose of proceeding to Brussels 3 Officers & 7 other ranks were sent from the Battalion and a very enjoyable time was spent.	
	" 6th		Voluntary Church Services as usual.	
	" 7th		There are no events of note to record today	
	" 8th		There are no events of note to record today.	
	" 9th		Lieut Bond M. C. proceeded for demobilization. A football match was played between the Battalion & 6th Somerset L.I. after a very strenuous game the final score was a draw of 2 goals each. R. S. M. Arlett. D. C. M. proceeded to Home Establishments.	
	10th		There are no events of note to record today.	H. Q. Sabul

D. D. & L., London, E.C. (A7883) Wt. W809/M1672 350,000 4/17 Sch. 52a Forms/C/2118/14

Instructions regarding War Diaries and Intelligence Summaries are contained in F. S. Regs., Part II. and the Staff Manual respectively. Title pages will be prepared in manuscript.

WAR DIARY
or
~~INTELLIGENCE SUMMARY.~~
(Erase heading not required.)

Army Form C. 2118.

Place	Date 1919	Hour	Summary of Events and Information	Remarks and references to Appendices
BERSEE	Apl 11th		There are no events of note to record today	
	" 12		" " " " " " " " "	
	" 13		Voluntary Church Services as usual.	
	" 14		There are no events of note to record today.	
	" 15		" " " " " " " " "	
	" 16		" " " " " " " " "	
	" 17		" " " " " " " " "	
	" 18		Another lorry was allotted to the Brigade Cadre for the purpose of proceeding to Brussels 3 Officers and 5 other ranks were sent from this Battalion, and after a very tiresome but somewhat dusty journey returned having thoroughly enjoyed themselves	
	" 19		There are no events of note to record today.	
	" 20		Voluntary Church Services as usual.	
			Capt H. H. Parker proceeded to U.K. for demobilization	
	" 21		There are no events of note to record today	
	22		" " " " " " " "	

D. D. & L., London, E.C.
(A7883) Wt W809/M1672 350,000 4/17 Sch 52a Forms/C/2118/14

Army Form C. 2118.

Instructions regarding War Diaries and Intelligence Summaries are contained in F. S. Regs., Part II. and the Staff Manual respectively. Title pages will be prepared in manuscript.

WAR DIARY
or
~~INTELLIGENCE SUMMARY.~~
(Erase heading not required.)

Place	Date 1919	Hour	Summary of Events and Information	Remarks and references to Appendices
BERSEE	Apl 22		There are no events of note to record today	
	" 23		" " " " " " " "	
	" 24		" " " " " " " "	
	" 25		" " " " " " " "	
	" 26		" " " " " " " "	
	" 27		Voluntary Church Services as usual.	
	" 28		Major G.C. Wetherall proceeded on leave to U.K.	
	29		There are no events of note to record today.	
	30		" " " " " " " "	

[signature]
LT. COL.
CDG. 18th BN. GLOUCESTERSHIRE REGT.

D. D. & L., London, E.C.
(A7883) Wt W809/M1672 350,000 4/17 Sch. 52a Forms/C/2118/14

Instructions regarding War Diaries and Intelligence Summaries are contained in F. S. Regs., Part II. and the Staff Manual respectively. Title pages will be prepared in manuscript.

WAR DIARY
or
~~INTELLIGENCE SUMMARY.~~
(Erase heading not required.)

Army Form C. 2118.

V.S. 10

Place	Date	Hour	Summary of Events and Information	Remarks and references to Appendices
BERSEE	1919 May 1st		There are no events of note to record today.	LR
	" 2		" " " " "	LR
	" 3		Voluntary Services as usual.	LR
	" 4		There are no events of note to record today.	LR
	" 5		" " " " "	LR
	" 6		A football match was played today between a team picked from the Cadres of the Brigade and the 7th Dragoons (French). The French team were victorious by 2 goals to none. In the evening the Officers of the 7th Dragoons were invited to dine with the Officers of the Battalion. The French Officers present were Col. Herbillon, Commandant D'Aumal, Capt Widelf, Aspirant Pasti. A very pleasant evening was spent.	LR
	7th		There are no events of note to record today.	LR
	8th		2/Lt. E. E. White proceeded for demobilization.	LR
	9th		The Cadre paraded at the Aerodrome at BERSEE at [illegible]7.45 hours to watch the review of the 7th Dragoons (French) by the kind invitation of Col. Herbillon.	LR

D. D. & L., London, E.C.
(A10266) Wt W5300/P713 750,000 2/18 Sch. 52 Forms/C2118/16.

Instructions regarding War Diaries and Intelligence Summaries are contained in F. S. Regs., Part II. and the Staff Manual respectively. Title pages will be prepared in manuscript.

WAR DIARY
or
~~INTELLIGENCE SUMMARY.~~
(Erase heading not required.)

Army Form C. 2118.

Place	Date 1919	Hour	Summary of Events and Information	Remarks and references to Appendices
	May 10th		Voluntary services as usual.	LR
	" 11th		There are no events of note to record today.	LR
	" 12th		" " " " " " " "	LR
	" 13th		" " " " " " " "	LR
	" 14th		" " " " " " " "	LR
	" 15th		" " " " " " " "	LR
	" 16th		" " " " " " " "	LR
	" 17th		Voluntary services as usual.	LR
	" 18th		Capt R. N. Addington M.C. proceeded for demobilization	LR
	" 19th		There are no events of note to record today	LR
	" 20		" " " " " " " "	LR
	" 21		" " " " " " " "	LR
	" 22		" " " " " " " "	LR
	" 23		Voluntary Services as usual	LR
	" 24		Major J. C. Wetherall rejoined from leave to U.K.	
			Lieut & Q.M. R. C. Dawson " " " "	LR
	" 25		There are no events of note to record today	LR
	" 26		Capt J. D. Heath proceeded on leave to U.K.	LR
	" 27		There are no events of note to record today	LR

D. D. & L., London, E.C. (A10266) Wt W5300/P713 750,000 2/18 Sch. 52 Forms/C2118/16.

Army Form C. 2118.

Instructions regarding War Diaries and Intelligence Summaries are contained in F. S. Regs., Part II. and the Staff Manual respectively. Title pages will be prepared in manuscript.

WAR DIARY
or
~~INTELLIGENCE SUMMARY.~~

(Erase heading not required.)

Place	Date 1919	Hour	Summary of Events and Information	Remarks and references to Appendices
BERSEE	May. 28		There are no events of note to record today	[illegible]
	29		" " " " " " " "	[illegible]
	30		" " " " " " " "	[illegible]
	31		The Cadre moved to TEMPLEUVE.	[illegible]

[illegible signature]
Major
Cmdg. 18th Bn Gloucester Regiment

D. D. & L., London, E.C.
(A10266) Wt W5300/P713 750,000 2/18 Sch. 52 Forms/C2118/16.

www.ingramcontent.com/pod-product-compliance
Lightning Source LLC
Chambersburg PA
CBHW081452160426
43193CB00013B/2458

* 9 7 8 1 4 7 4 5 2 3 3 7 0 *